Make it Vegan

Make it Vegan

Simple Plant-based
Recipes for Everyone

Madeleine Olivia

Photography by Ali Green
and Clare Winfield

Hardie Grant
BOOKS

About
Maddie

Growing up in Cornwall, I was surrounded by countryside. Living with chickens, cats, dogs and hamsters and with cows on the doorstep in the adjoining fields. I have a mum who adores cooking and has a collection of cookbooks unlike any other, and a dad who is passionate about nature and the outdoors. During my childhood I always found comfort and happiness in food. My mum encouraged us to cook our own food from scratch and made delicious home-cooked meals every night. I spent a lot of my time outdoors, making silly videos with my sister, singing, dancing and playing. In hindsight it makes me laugh that making skits and mini vlogs with my sister was our favourite thing to do, and now it's my job.

I enjoyed learning as a teenager, and so when I couldn't make the decision about what I wanted to be when I grew up, I mixed two of my favourite subjects, art and history, and decided to apply to university for Art History. I travelled across the UK to study at St Andrews in Scotland, where I had lots of fun drinking, and slightly less fun actually studying my chosen subject. About halfway through my time at university I realised the conventional trajectory post-uni of getting a big job in the city just wasn't for me. I had a difficult time during my uni years, developing an eating disorder and feeling like I didn't fit in. In my last year I went vegan, after finding comfort in watching YouTubers online who sold the vegan dream to me. Initially it was the lure of a new diet, but my motivations for being vegan changed when I learned more about what it stood for.

MAKE IT VEGAN

When I graduated, I returned home and attempted (and failed) to start a career in Cornwall. Art galleries wouldn't have me due to lack of experience, so I was cleaning hotel rooms for a while, working part-time for a Cornish magazine and part-time as a marketing assistant for a holiday park. It turns out I still hadn't figured out what I wanted to be when I grew up. This was all while continuing my university drinking habits. It reached a point in 2016 where I had a quarter-life crisis, quit my job, quit drinking and moved back home to try and figure my life out.

It was during this time that I started my YouTube channel. I had been obsessed with YouTube ever since it started, and I preferred winding down in the evening to my favourite content creators' vlogs over actual television. I had always wanted to post videos online, but never had the confidence. Now I was at a crossroads in my life, and with my newfound passion for veganism, minimalism and sustainability, I wanted to share my experiences through this new outlet. I fantasised about it becoming my job, but was so surprised when I started to make money sharing my advice and learnings online. I attracted a community of likeminded people who also wanted to go vegan, declutter their wardrobes, try natural beauty products and live more sustainably.

After some time travelling in Southeast Asia, my husband Alex and I returned to the UK and rented a flat in Brighton. We then made the decision to try and grow the business together. With an extra helping hand we were successful in producing higher quality content and growing my audience. After a year in Brighton and a newfound career, we decided to return to Cornwall and buy a home, after our risks and hard work had paid off. I filmed our renovations, budget vegan food shops, mental health struggles, quick and easy recipes, getting engaged, writing my first book, adopting our dog Roxie, moving house, getting married and everything in between.

That roughly brings me to today, where I am writing my very first cookbook; a dream of mine ever since I started sharing recipes. After sharing recipes online for so long, it is incredible that I am now able to share them in print. I can only hope that in making veganism accessible through my simple and easy recipes, I can get more people eating more plants!

MAKE IT VEGAN

Why Vegan?

During university I tried every diet there was. Unfortunately, this meant I dealt with an eating disorder where I became vulnerable to outside messages from the media around diet culture. Being away from home, studying for a degree in a high-pressured environment and struggling to be myself and connect with people made me seek control elsewhere: through my diet. In my last year of university, I came across one more diet: veganism. During that time online, veganism became popular through diet fads that attracted people like me with a disordered relationship with food. I quickly ditched my meat-eating habits, and went vegan overnight.

In many ways, going vegan put me onto the path to recovery, by enabling me to let go of many limiting beliefs around food and calories, and learning how to cook plant-based food in new and tasty ways. It became a passion of mine. After some time, I learned more about the health benefits, the impact of animal agriculture on the environment, and the awful atrocities that happen all over the world to farmed animals, giving me the motivation to make this a full lifestyle change.

However, in my first few years of being vegan, I was following a restrictive vegan diet. As with all diets I'd tried, I failed and beat myself up for not being able to keep it up, and therefore seeing myself as just not good enough. This is the oldest trick in the book when it comes to diet culture, so I'll save you the experimentation and tell you that it's the diet that's the problem, not you. I look back now and realise I was experiencing orthorexia (an unhealthy obsession with clean eating) and had replaced one eating disorder with another. I am therefore passionate about removing diet culture from veganism. I am adamant that veganism doesn't need to be restrictive. As a vegan, I'll also be the first to say you don't have to go fully vegan if that doesn't work for you. What we eat, after all, is deeply entrenched in our cultures and lifestyle, and so changing this is complex.

A turning point since going vegan was when I decided to completely reject diet culture as a whole, and instead live my life according to my own rules. Eating foods that made my body feel good, that matched my morals, and arguably most importantly, that I enjoyed eating. I am happy to say that after all these years and a lot of hard work, therapy and self-reflection, I remain vegan for moral and environmental reasons, but enjoy all the meat alternatives and veganised recipes as a part of a balanced diet.

A huge reason I remain vegan, and maintain a passion for cooking with plants, is reducing my food footprint and hopefully inspiring others to do the same. This includes the catastrophic harm the animal food industry is having on the environment, on animals and on people. I never took the time to consider where my food really came from before going vegan. I have since learned how intensive livestock farming is, making it a leading contributor to greenhouse gas emissions. Not only that, but animal agriculture hugely contributes to deforestation, species extinction, ocean dead zones, water pollution and habitat destruction. This level of intensity in farming has taken over the industry, where 'improved efficiency' is code for smaller living spaces, more pesticides and increasingly reduced care for the billions of animals that are being commodified each year.

The human impact is also vast, meaning marginalised groups all across the world are working in inhumane and unethical environments in order to meet the demand, as well as being the most impacted by the environmental damage caused by overfishing and overfarming. Plants aren't exempt from these unethical food chains either, making it even more important to source ingredients as locally and seasonally as possible. Learning this showed me how our food systems need to change dramatically. And while the responsibility doesn't sit solely on the shoulders of the individual, but the industries using these practices, it is something that I could choose not to support. Whether you choose to go completely vegan, simply eat more plants, learn where your food comes from, or eat seasonally and source locally, it all makes a big difference.

INTRODUCTION

About
the Book

It's been my dream for a long time to write a cookbook. Food is my passion, and one of the things that going vegan has gifted me is experimenting with cooking. Getting creative in the kitchen is my favourite thing to do, whether that's figuring out how to replicate the texture of cheese, or make mushrooms taste delicious to a mushroom-hater. I love to know where my food comes from and to make dishes from scratch. Sharing the fruits of this labour with my family, friends and those online who watch my cooking videos is one of life's biggest joys.

With this book I want to make vegan food accessible to everyone, including non-vegans. I want to share that it doesn't need to be restrictive or extreme. My ultimate goal is to help you learn how to cook more with plants and incorporate more vegetables, fruits, grains and pulses (legumes) into your life. Eating more plants can provide extra nutrients, flavours and variety in everyone's existing diet. It's about adding over removing, enjoying over restricting, experimenting over repeating.

The recipes in this book are ones from my childhood, adapted versions of my favourite meals growing up, or inspired by my time spent in other countries eating their delicious food. There are many that I just wanted to veganise! I want to take out the complications of being vegan which can make it feel unattainable or impossible. Ultimately, we could all do with including more vegan meals and trialling new

ingredients and dishes in our weekly meal plans. This will not only benefit our health and be more sustainable and ethical than buying pre-packaged, animal-based and highly processed food, but also help us to slow down in our day-to-day lives. Getting in the kitchen is like therapy to me! It's a moment in my day that I can put on some Norah Jones, stop looking at my phone and create something delicious.

Growing up with a mum who loved to cook and could start a library of cookbooks because she has so many, I feel very lucky. Her influence on me and my way of cooking is huge. I feel so grateful that in learning about different cuisines that are enjoyed across the world through her knowledge of cooking, I've been able to implement this into my recipes. I am a true believer in appreciating different cultures and

INTRODUCTION

their ways of cooking and eating, because we have a lot to learn from each other. Tasting foods from different cultures in recipes that have been developed over centuries, and created through love within families and communities, is a huge privilege I never take for granted. What has been so enriching over the last decade of being vegan, has been discovering just how much vegetarian and vegan food is loved all over the world. I therefore wanted to bring this admiration for all kinds of cuisines into this book.

The foundation of my recipes is simplicity. Making them achievable for someone who is coming home from work tired. Making them accessible to someone with a disability. Making them easy for someone new to cooking. Whatever place you're starting at with a curiosity for vegan food, I want to simplify things so that it doesn't become overwhelming to the point of giving up. Learning the skill of cooking can be hard in adulthood if it wasn't taught to you when you were younger, just as finding the time to make dishes from scratch can feel impossible with a busy schedule and many responsibilities. So, while sometimes that means cutting corners or removing steps, it can also mean making the time to fit cooking into your life. Most of my recipes are extremely adaptable and I do that to encourage you to get creative in the kitchen. As far as I am aware you aren't running a restaurant, nor being judged on *MasterChef*, so let go of any pressure you have for perfecting each recipe you create, and just keep it simple. Nobody else can tell you how to enjoy your food. I therefore want to empower you to make it how you like.

We are all aware of the incredible health benefits of a diet rich in fruits, vegetables and legumes, but that doesn't mean it needs to become dogmatic. Leave behind the concepts of purity, 'clean eating' or cutting things

out of your life. A 'healthy' lifestyle isn't one that removes the fun out of food, or one that leaves you hungry, tired, moody and miserable because of a restrictive diet. Vegan, plant-based, flexitarian, vegetarian, whatever you want to call it, can be a diet filled with richness and variety that includes salads and brownies. In this book you'll find green smoothies because they're packed full of juicy nutrients that make our bodies feel good, pastas because they taste heavenly, cakes to share with family and soups because they warm our tummies. Just because they are vegan doesn't mean they have to be 'clean', or follow any prescriptive measures, beyond not including animal products. That's my motivation for these recipes: to provide inspiration and ideas for those choosing to remove or reduce animal products because they want to for their own personal, moral or ethical stance, not because they feel they have to in order to follow a diet fad.

For all of the recipes I've included whether they're gluten-, soy-, or nut-free for those with allergies or intolerances, as well as lots of information about how the recipes can be varied with different ingredients. I share the ways in which you can substitute common animal-based foods and also how to swap out ingredients in recipes so they work to fit the seasons or what you have in your cupboards. I also recommend pantry and kitchen essentials and give you my best tips for saving money and effort with meal planning and prepping. My hope is that the recipes will get you started with veganism or push you further along the path of plant-based cooking.

Meal Prep

Recently, I started to properly plan and meal prep for the week. I'm not talking about the boring meal prep you sometimes see, featuring an entire week of rice, broccoli and unseasoned protein. Who wants to eat the exact same thing every day for every meal? Instead, I mean deciding on a variety of delicious dishes you're going to eat that week, and prepping some quick options at the weekend to grab for breakfast, lunch and snacks throughout the week.
I find that not only does it take less time to prepare the food than I expect it to (usually 1–1½ hours), but it sets me up for success during the week. It means I eat lots of vegetables and have more time to relax during my lunch breaks, and it also reduces my food waste. More than this, it seriously reduces the mental labour of having to think about what to eat for every meal. I've also found it creates the opportunity to eat a wider variety of foods, eat more seasonally, save money by using what I have in my cupboards and refrigerator and try out new recipes!

CREATE A SYSTEM

Before you begin, decide on a system that works best for you and your kitchen. I often use an app called AnyList to plan my weekly menu and create a shopping list, alongside a website called EatYourBooks where I can log all my cookbook recipes to import. But often, it is simplest to start with a good old pen and paper, or the notes app on your phone. There are also meal planning notepads designed exactly for this purpose with a shopping list section. Whatever you decide to use, just choose something that is simple and sustainable.

MAKE IT VEGAN

DECIDING RECIPES BASED ON WHAT YOU ALREADY HAVE TO HAND

Start by having a look in the refrigerator and see what ingredients need to be eaten. You probably have a jar of something that's been in there for a while, or some vegetables that are on their last legs. Next, look in your cupboards and see if there is anything that has been there for a long time, or something you're really craving! Finally, check the freezer for anything that could be used for a quick meal. This will reduce food waste, save you money and keep your cupboards tidy.

STORECUPBOARD, REFRIGERATOR AND FREEZER STOCKLIST

An extension of this if you really want to get organised (this is not for everyone) is to create a stocklist. Go through your food and write everything down. Again, I'm sure there are apps for this! You could stick with noting the basics you always buy, or literally write down absolutely everything you have. Doing it digitally, on an app or Word document or spreadsheet, will make it simpler to update. You can amend this once a week based on the meal plan you made and use it as a starting point to see which foods you want to cook with (without having to look through the cupboards every week). When you're out and about you can also reference it to see what you do or don't have at home.

SAVE RECIPES FROM BOOKS AND ONLINE

Once you have your system decided and you've checked your stocks, you can start browsing recipes. I have lots of amazing vegan cookbooks (and now I have my own!), but I also have recipes saved on AnyList, Pinterest, Instagram or TikTok. Choose one or two new or fun ones and add those to your weekly plan. This is helpful for using ingredients you already have, and also to try something new.

CHOOSING BASIC RECIPES YOU KNOW AND LOVE

With that being said, I'd recommend you don't overwhelm yourself with lots of new recipes. Stick to one or two a week. Especially if you're new to cooking, meal planning or meal prepping. Bulk the week out mainly with the recipes you know and love, or even vegan versions of your favourite meals like the ones in this book. That way you're doing things gradually, and over time you'll be adding more meals to your roster.

MEAL PREP VS MEAL PLAN

What will you be meal prepping ahead of the week? What will you be cooking on the day? On a Sunday I try and meal prep lunches for the following working week, a few breakfasts and maybe a snack or sweet and one dinner. Most of the dinners I'll cook on the day and make enough for leftovers the next day. Everyone is different, so decide what works best for you.

WRITE IT DOWN

Now you can write it all down and organise it day by day. I always start with what I'll be having for breakfast as it is usually very similar day to day, week to week (overnight oats, bircher muesli, or my Baked One-pan Scramble, page 43). Then I decide on meal prep for lunch (a soup, stew, curry, salad, roasted vegetables, etc.) and if I want to make any snacks or sweets (breakfast bars, protein bars, cakes, biscuits/

cookies). Finally, I'll write my menu for dinners. Once the meal plan is in place, you can then compile a shopping list. This is one of the reasons I love using an app, as it creates a shopping list for you based on your menu for the week.

BATCH COOKING

I'd recommend batch cooking at least one recipe a week. This can be a soup, stew, chilli, curry, pasta sauce, slow-cooked recipe or some kind of gratin. For example, my Spinach and Butter Bean Soup (page 64), Pasta all Norma (page 92), Tofu Satay Curry (page 102), Parmigiana Melanzane (page 95), or Celeriac Gratin (Dauphinoise) (page 160). This can be eaten as lunch throughout the week, served with different accompaniments on different days and even frozen to defrost at a later date. It also makes the meal prepping process simpler if you're cooking everything in one large saucepan.

STORAGE

Make sure you have the right containers to store your food in. I mainly use jars, glass and plastic containers, and silicone bags. The jars are good for salad dressings, juices, overnight oats or bircher muesli. Plastic and glass containers are the most universally used for storage in the refrigerator and cupboards, for portioning foods out and storing leftovers. Silicone bags are handy for portions of soup, breadcrumbs, homemade sweet treats or for taking out as a packed lunch.

REDUCING FOOD WASTE

One of the biggest motivations for me beyond eating healthily, cooking at home and saving money is reducing the food waste and consumption in our home. Around one-third of food on the planet is wasted, and that is due to our throwaway and fast-paced culture. Slowing it down a little and taking the time to plan means you're able to limit food waste at home.

Kitchen Essentials:
Equipment

If all you have in your kitchen is a knife, cutting board, pans and utensils, then you can still cook up a storm. You don't need specialised equipment, but it can really help to expand the foods you're able to create and cook at home. Here are the pieces of equipment I love and use in my kitchen every day or every week. While they aren't essential, they're definitely all very helpful.

CAKE AND LOAF TINS

Having a couple of cake and loaf tins (pans) is important for vegan baking! The springform kind of round cake tins with removable bases are especially handy to pop open when the cake is ready.

CAST-IRON PANS

Invest in a set of cast-iron pans if you can – they are my favourite to cook with. They'll last a lifetime, are consistent and have an enamel coating that stops things sticking.

CERAMIC GRATIN DISH

For traybakes and hearty casseroles, you can't beat a ceramic gratin dish. I have them in many different sizes for a variety of uses.

CITRUS JUICER

I have a hand-held one that gets every last drop out of a lemon, lime or orange, leaving the seeds behind. Seeing as I like to use lemon in most meals, it is an item I use pretty much every day.

WIRE RACK

Essential to pop your freshly baked loaf of bread or cake on to cool once it's removed from the oven.

STAND-UP COLANDER

You'll need a sturdy colander to rest in the sink to drain anything you've been cooking in water, or to rinse off your fruit and vegetables.

DOUGH SCRAPER

For making your own bread, a dough scraper is a must. My favourite is a plastic one, as you can use it on any work surface and it is more bendable than a metal one for scraping the dough out of a bowl or from a work surface.

FOOD PROCESSOR

Alongside a blender, a food processor isn't used as much in my kitchen, but it is really helpful when making dips and sauces like hummus or vegan pesto, pastry or crumble or when creating your own homemade burgers or my Black Bean Meatballs (page 96).

If you can't yet afford a large food processor or blender, then opting for a smaller version can save you money and gives you the opportunity to blend things up easily. I have both a big and small one mainly out of convenience and also to save on washing-up if I'm just blending a small amount.

GARLIC PRESS

Finely chopping garlic with a knife is annoying when you use garlic in basically every single recipe. There are a million different types of garlic press, but my favourite is a hand-held one where there are no removable parts.

GOOD-QUALITY KNIVES AND SHARPENER

Having different knives to use for cutting your ingredients is very important if you want to make your cooking easier and more enjoyable. You don't need to spend a fortune, just make sure they are good quality and sharpened regularly.

MAKE IT VEGAN

NON-STICK PAN

Ideal for pancakes, roasting nuts or making toasties, and when cooking with non-dairy milk, having even just one non-stick pan is essential for the kitchen. Opt for ones without any harmful chemicals.

IMMERSION BLENDER

To save having to tip your soups into a blender and then back into the pan, get yourself an immersion blender. It's not only a lot cheaper but creates less washing-up. Many come with multiple different attachments to use for soups, sauces, smoothies and pastes.

VITAMIX BLENDER

I've had a couple of blenders in the past, but nothing beats my Vitamix. It was a dream when I got it as a birthday present from my husband, Alex, and I use it constantly. Nothing can get sauces smoother. With that being said, any blender is a good idea in the kitchen, whatever the price, to blend ingredients for recipes.

MANDOLIN

An ultra-sharp device to slice potatoes and vegetables super thin for dishes like Celeriac Gratin (Dauphinoise) (page 160).

MEASURING CUPS OR JUGS

Get yourself a set of measuring cups, including tablespoon and teaspoon measures, and a measuring jug with the measurements on it. This can simplify certain recipes to save you bringing out the scales. If you're clumsy, save the ceramic ones for display and get yourself some metal ones instead.

MICROPLANE

For zesting, grating whole spices, vegan cheese, garlic and ginger and even chocolate decorating. Alongside my citrus juicer and garlic press, I use a microplane most days.

MINI WHISK

This comes in handy more often than you'd think, as you can use it to make gravy extra smooth, for a matcha tea or to remove the lumps from white sauces. I have both a metal and silicone one (for using on non-stick pans).

STAND MIXER

If you're committed to vegan baking, then a stand mixer is going to make your life a lot easier. It saves having to knead dough and makes cake batter come together quickly without the arm ache.

KITCHEN SCISSORS

Sometimes snipping things is just easier than chopping them with a knife. Plus, it's a lot safer to open packaging with a pair of scissors than a sharp knife you're using to chop your vegetables. Buy a pair that dismantles for easy cleaning.

SILICONE SPATULA

A silicone spatula is extremely useful in the kitchen and has so many uses, including getting every last bit of cookie dough out of the bowl, scraping down the sides when you're blending in a food processor, and decorating your cake with icing (frosting).

SILICONE MAT

Instead of needing to repurchase baking parchment constantly, purchase a few silicone sheets for your baking trays (pans) and baking sheets that are washable and therefore reusable. I still use baking parchment occasionally for cakes or certain dishes that require it, but day to day I exclusively use the silicone sheets to line trays and sheets to stop food from sticking.

STAINLESS-STEEL MIXING BOWLS

For food preparation and baking, a collection of different sized mixing bowls will be used every week as you start cooking more.

STORAGE CONTAINERS

Bowls, plastic containers, glass containers, jars, boxes, etc., are essential in a kitchen for meal prepping, storing and keeping your food. I have a variety that have been handed down to me, bought new or picked up in charity shops secondhand.

SPICE TIN

I love using an Indian spice tin to store all of my essential spices in one place. It makes it easier to cook dishes that need multiple spices without having to get them all out individually!

EASY VEGETABLE PEELER

For meal prep, a vegetable peeler is a must-have. Find a wide Y-shaped, sharp one that makes it quick and easy to prep your vegetables and saves any accidents when using a knife.

WOOD CUTTING BOARD

I only have wood cutting boards in my kitchen as they are easy to clean, won't dull your knives and double up as serving boards.

—

Building up a stocked storecupboard will be important in your endeavours when cooking with plants. Over the following pages are all the categories of foods I think are ideal to keep in your kitchen cupboard so you can create different dishes and also experiment with cooking. Beyond the basics, some are more specialist or unusual, which are fun to try from time to time.

INTRODUCTION

Kitchen Essentials: *Ingredients*

GRAINS

Grains are essential to keep you full, give you energy and accompany vegetables and pulses (legumes). The more variety, the better!

— Wheat (bread, flour, pastry, pasta, noodles)
— Rice (brown, red, wild, white, jasmine, basmati, arborio, long-grain)
— Corn (popcorn, polenta/cornmeal, corn tortillas)
— Oats
— Ancient grains (quinoa, amaranth, kamut, spelt, freekeh, farro, millet, sorghum, teff, barley, rye, burghul)

PULSES

A vital source of protein in a vegan diet, and some of the most nutritious foods on the planet, make sure you eat and include a variety of pulses (legumes) in your storecupboard.

— Soybean (tofu, tempeh, edamame beans)
— Beans (chickpeas/garbanzos, kidney beans, borlotti/cranberry beans, butter/lima beans, pinto beans, black-eyed peas, broad/fava beans, haricot beans, cannellini beans, mung beans, adzuki beans)
— Lentils (Puy lentils, red lentils, green lentils, yellow lentils, black beluga lentils)

NUTS AND SEEDS

High in essential fatty acids and protein, nuts and seeds are ideal for vegan baking and as a snack, or in butter form. I try to eat some form of nuts or seeds every day.

— Nuts (cashews, walnuts, almonds, peanuts, pistachios, pecans, hazelnuts, brazils, macadamias, pine)
— Seeds (pumpkin, sunflower, chia, flax, sesame, poppy, hemp, caraway)
— Nut and seed butters (peanut butter, almond butter, cashew butter, tahini)

DRIED FRUITS

Having dried fruits in the cupboard is ideal for vegan baking, as a snack or to top your granola in the morning.

— Stone fruits (Medjool dates, apricots, prunes, mango, figs)
— Raisins, sultanas (golden raisins), currants
— Berries (goji berries, cranberries, cherries)
— Coconut (desiccated/dried shredded, flaked, toasted)

OILS

I mainly use extra virgin olive oil because we all know how good it is for you, but I still use other vegetable oils for different reasons, whether that's deep-frying with rapeseed (canola) oil or drizzling sesame oil over my stir-fry.

— Extra virgin olive oil/olive oil
— Vegetable oils (rapeseed/canola, sunflower oil, avocado oil)
— Coconut oil
— Toasted sesame oil

VINEGARS

The acid in vinegars gives depth of flavour to many recipes. They can also be used in vegan baking to help batters rise.

— Balsamic vinegar
— Red/white wine vinegar
— Apple cider vinegar
— Rice vinegar

HERBS

Fresh or dried, herbs will bring increased flavour and added nutrients to your meals. Dried oregano or mixed herbs (usually an Italian mix) are the ones I use the most regularly, while for fresh I always have coriander (cilantro) in the refrigerator.

— Mixed herbs
— Oregano
— Thyme
— Sage
— Rosemary
— Bay leaves (best dried)
— Basil
— Chives
— Coriander (cilantro)
— Parsley
— Dill
— Lemongrass

SPICES AND SEASONING

Not only are spices going to make your food sing, but they're seriously good for you. They're wonderful for vegan cooking, especially as vegan protein can have a milder flavour than animal products.

MAKE IT VEGAN

- Anise
- Allspice
- Asafoetida
- Black pepper
- Caraway seeds
- Cardamom
- Cayenne powder
- Chilli powder or chilli (hot pepper) flakes
- Cinnamon
- Clove
- Coriander powder/seeds
- Cumin powder/seeds
- Curry powder
- Fennel seeds
- Fenugreek
- Garam masala
- Garlic powder or granules
- Ground coriander/coriander seeds
- Ground cumin/cumin seeds
- Nigella seeds/black mustard seeds
- Nutmeg
- Onion powder
- Paprika
- Ras el hanout
- Saffron
- Smoked paprika
- Turmeric (fresh or ground)

TINNED FOODS

I always have tinned tomatoes and coconut milk in my storecupboard. They're the base of many of my dishes and can keep for long periods of time. Plus, tinned vegetables and fruits are a great backup when you run out of fresh.

- Tinned tomatoes (chopped, passata/sieved tomatoes, purée/paste, plum)
- Coconut milk/cream

- Tinned vegetables (sweetcorn, potatoes, mushrooms, peas, baby carrots, mixed vegetables)
- Tinned fruit (peaches, apricots, pears, prunes, peach slices, pineapple chunks, mandarin, grapefruit)

CONDIMENTS

There are lots of condiments that are unfortunately not vegan friendly. The following are the ones that live in my storecupboard and refrigerator at all times and are totally plant based.

- Soy sauce
- Tomato ketchup
- Barbecue sauce
- Mustard
- Hot sauce (sriracha, sweet chilli, Tabasco, piri piri, Cholula Mexican sauce)
- Wasabi
- Vegan mayonnaise
- Jam
- Marmite

PICKLED FOODS

We love a pickle or a gherkin, and fermented foods are a great source of probiotics (healthy bacteria) for the gut. I usually have some form of pickles in my refrigerator and love to make my own!

- Sauerkraut
- Vegan kimchi (check for fish)
- Gherkins
- Pickled onions

SUGAR, SWEETENERS AND BAKING

We don't need to shy away from sugars if we are healthy. Sugars can add sweetness and flavour to cakes and desserts that can be a part of a balanced diet. Again, I always have these in my storecupboard so I can always bake something when I fancy it!

— Sugars (light brown, dark brown, white granulated, caster/superfine)
— Syrups (maple, agave, golden/light corn, molasses)
— Flavourings (vanilla extract)
— Chocolate (cocoa/unsweetened chocolate powder, raw cacao powder, vegan dark chocolate with at least 70% cocoa solids, vegan milk chocolate)

FLOUR AND RISING AGENTS

A necessity for all types of baking, from bread to cakes to brownies, and even for thickening sauces.

— Flour (strong bread flour, plain/all-purpose flour, self-raising/self-rising flour, wholemeal/wholewheat flour, rye flour, gluten-free flour, cornflour/cornstarch)
— Bicarbonate of soda (baking soda)
— Baking powder
— Fast-action yeast

VEGAN ALTERNATIVES

These aren't necessarily essential, but I usually buy some during my weekly food shop, such as non-dairy milks for my teas and coffees, and vegan alternatives when I'm craving a cheeseburger.

— TVP (textured vegetable protein, which is made from soy and works great as a high-protein meat alternative)
— Shop-bought vegan meat alternatives
— Seitan (a vegan meat alternative made from gluten – see page 110 for how to make from scratch)
— Non-dairy milks (soy, oat, coconut, rice, pea, cashew, almond, hemp)
— Vegan cheeses
— Vegan butters and plant-based spreads
— Vegan creams, yoghurts and ice creams

INTRODUCTION

MAKE IT VEGAN

SPECIALIST INGREDIENTS

These ingredients aren't essential but are things I always have in my storecupboard. If you're committing to a fully vegan diet, or to eating a lot more plant-based food, then they are items I'd recommend you try, so you can experiment with different unique flavours. Many of them can be found in the supermarket, or if not, online.

— Nutritional yeast – a great source of vitamin B12 and can be added to dishes to give them a cheesy flavour.
— Aquafaba – the liquid from a tin of chickpeas (garbanzos), which can be used in vegan baking and to make vegan meringue.

— Agar agar powder – the vegan alternative to gelatine. This ingredient will act as a jelly to set homemade vegan tofu (see No-feta Greek Inspired Salad, page 150).
— Chickpea (gram) flour – a common ingredient in Indian cooking that works amazingly to mimic egg dishes.
— Liquid smoke – adds depth of flavour and a barbecued smokiness to vegan dishes looking to imitate meat.
— *Kala namak*/black salt – a sulphurous salt that can be used on top of my Baked One-pan Scramble (page 43), omelettes and 'egg' recipes. I buy mine online as it is not readily available in supermarkets.
— Agave syrup – a vegan sweet alternative to honey.
— Jackfruit – this fruit tears apart like meat, and can be fantastic mixed with barbecue seasoning.
— Miso – adds the umami to a recipe and is full of nutrients due to its fermentation.
— Vital wheat gluten – just the gluten from flour used to make seitan: a vegan meat alternative (page 110).
— Nori – dried seaweed commonly used for sushi and packed with iodine. It can be used as a way to bring the flavours of the sea to a dish without using fish or seafood.

36-55

Wake

Up

Baked One-pan Scramble p. 43

Smoothies p. 44

Ultimate Porridge p. 48

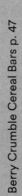

Berry Crumble Cereal Bars p. 47

Vegan Omelette p. 40.

Maple Pancakes p. 50

Plant-based Pains au Chocolat p. 54

Marmalady Muffins p. 53

Vegan Omelette

Chickpea (gram) flour is a magic ingredient for vegan egg-inspired recipes. It is a staple in Indian cooking and often used for a *besan chilla* (savoury pancake). This recipe can be adapted in so many ways by using whatever vegetables you fancy, adding some vegan cheese and serving not just for breakfast, but for lunch or dinner, too. With the addition of *kala namak* (black salt) it can create an eggy taste. It is also naturally gluten- and soy-free, plus high in protein!

MAKES 1 OMELETTE

—

PREP TIME 10 MINS
COOK TIME 10 MINS

30 g (1 oz/¼ cup) chickpea (gram) flour
1 tablespoon nutritional yeast
¼ teaspoon *kala namak* (black salt) for a more egg-like flavour or use ordinary sea salt, plus extra to serve
freshly ground black pepper
75 ml (2½ fl oz/5 tablespoons) water
2 tablespoons olive oil
small handful of chopped parsley, to serve

OPTIONAL
handful of vegetables, such as mushrooms, spring onions (scallion), broccoli, cavolo nero, peas, spinach, tomato and (bell) peppers, finely chopped
sprinkle of chopped herbs
handful of grated vegan cheese
sprinkle of chilli (hot pepper) flakes

1. Mix the chickpea flour, nutritional yeast, black salt (if using) or ordinary salt, and a grind of black pepper in a large bowl. Gradually whisk in the measured water until the mixture has a smooth consistency.

2. Heat the olive oil in a large frying pan over a medium heat, then pour in the mixture, gently swirling the pan to spread it out. You can also add a small sprinkle of chopped herbs, grated vegan cheese and chilli flakes if you like.

3. Fry one side until golden brown (you'll know it's done when the edges start to come away and bubbles are forming in the omelette, around 4–6 minutes). Flip the omelette over, add the chopped vegetables, if using, then flip half the omelette over to cover the other side and cook for a few more minutes. Serve with a sprinkling of parsley and extra black salt.

Baked One-pan Scramble

SERVES 2

—

PREP TIME 5 MINS
COOK TIME 25-30 MINS

Tofu is great for a vegan diet as it is high in protein, absorbs flavour well and can be cooked in a huge variety of ways. For this scramble, instead of frying everything in a pan, we're going to bake the tofu and vegetables in the oven. This is a fabulous dish to make ahead of time and tastes great topped with avocado, hot sauce and fresh herbs.

5 cherry tomatoes, halved
¼ red onion, thinly sliced
handful of spinach
400 g (14 oz) block of tofu
½ teaspoon ground turmeric
½ teaspoon ground cumin
½ teaspoon paprika
1 tablespoon soy sauce
2 tablespoons unsweetened
  non-dairy milk
40 g (1½ oz/2 cups) or about
  2 handfuls of breadcrumbs (or
  gluten-free breadcrumbs)
2 tablespoons nutritional yeast
olive oil, for drizzling
salt and freshly ground black
  pepper

OPTIONAL
handful of grated vegan cheese
pinch of *kala namak* (black salt)

1. Preheat a fan oven to 180°C (400°F).
2. Add the tomatoes and red onion to a small gratin dish. Tear in the spinach and crumble over the block of tofu with your hands. Sprinkle over the spices, drizzle in the soy sauce and non-dairy milk, season with salt and pepper, and mix everything together.
3. Sprinkle the breadcrumbs and nutritional yeast over the top, then drizzle with olive oil and sprinkle over the grated vegan cheese and black salt (if using).
4. Bake in the oven for 25–30 minutes until golden brown. Serve.

TIPS
— Other great veggie options are sliced mushrooms, broccoli, (bell) peppers, courgettes (zucchini) or kale.
— If you want a classic scrambled tofu, skip the gratin dish and fry everything up in a large frying pan (vegetables first until softened, then add the tofu and remaining ingredients). Omit the breadcrumbs and serve on top of toast.

Smoothies

Smoothies, next to porridge, are my go-to breakfast. They're quick to throw together and an easy way to get lots of healthy fruit, vegetables, nuts and seeds into your diet. There are endless combinations to make, but here are a few delicious ones to try in the morning. Adjust the measurements to your preference, in particular the amounts of liquid to make it thicker or runnier. I never measure the liquid out, but instead fill the blender until it is covering all the ingredients.

SERVES 1
—
PREP TIME 5 MINS

1 scoop vegan unflavoured
  or vanilla protein powder
120–250 ml (4–8 fl oz/½–1 cup)
  non-dairy milk
120–250 ml (4–8 fl oz/
  ½–1 cup) water
1 banana
handful of frozen berries
1 tablespoon chia seeds
1 tablespoon flaxseeds

1. Add all of the ingredients to the blender, blitz and serve.

TIPS:
— For a Chocolate Smoothie, add a 200 g (10½ oz) packet of silken tofu, 1 tablespoon of cocoa (unsweetened chocolate or raw cacao) powder, 2–3 Medjool dates, stoned, 1 tablespoon of flaxseeds, a handful of ice, 60–120 ml (2–4 fl oz/¼–½ cup) of non-dairy milk, ½ teaspoon of vanilla extract and an optional shot of espresso to the blender.
— If you fancy a Piña Mojito Smoothie, add ½ a pineapple, a handful of baby spinach, ¼ cucumber, a sprig of mint, grated zest and juice of ½ a lime, 120 ml (4 fl oz/½ cup) of coconut milk and 120 ml (4 fl oz/½ cup) of water to the blender.

MAKE IT VEGAN

Berry Crumble Cereal Bars

MAKES 16
—
PREP TIME 1 HOUR 20 MINS
COOK TIME 35 MINS

Inspired by a favourite pudding growing up, apple and blackberry crumble, these cereal bars are seriously more-ish. The berry jam in the middle adds sweetness, flavour and vitamins. Perfect for a quick grab-and-go breakfast, or with a cup of tea in the afternoon. Plus, you can also use any leftover berry chia jam to top your porridge, toast or vegan coconut yoghurt in the morning.

FOR THE CRUMBLE
280 g (10 oz/2¾ cups)
   rolled oats
180 g (6½ oz/1 cup) Medjool
   dates, stoned
80 ml (3 fl oz/⅓–¼ cup) maple
   syrup or use agave syrup
1 teaspoon ground cinnamon
60 ml (2 fl oz/¼ cup) coconut oil
½ teaspoon vanilla extract
splash of non-dairy milk
   (optional)

FOR THE BERRY CHIA JAM
200 g (7 oz/1⅔ cup) fresh or
   frozen berries
1 tablespoon maple syrup
1 tablespoon chia seeds
grated zest and juice of ½ lemon

OPTIONAL
handful of mixed seeds

1. Preheat a fan oven to 180°C (400°F). Grease a baking tray (pan) and line with baking parchment or a silicone sheet.
2. Add all the crumble ingredients to a food processor and blitz until they come together to form a crumbly dough.
3. Add two-thirds of the mixture to the baking tray and press down firmly with the back of a spoon to fill the tray. Leave to set in the refrigerator while you make the berry chia jam.
4. Make the berry chia jam by adding all the ingredients to a saucepan over a medium heat. Cook, stirring, for 5 minutes, mashing the berries as they soften, until slightly reduced. Don't worry too much if the jam is still runny, as it will thicken up in the oven.
5. Remove the baking tray from the refrigerator and pour over the jam. Top with the remaining crumble mixture. You can also add a sprinkle of seeds for added goodness and crunch.
6. Bake in the oven for 30 minutes, or until golden brown. Once cooked, leave to cool in the baking tray for 5–10 minutes, then transfer to a wire rack for about 1 hour, or until the crumble reaches room temperature before cutting into 16 bars.

TIPS
— Make sure you leave the bars to cool completely before slicing as this will stop them from crumbling. Plus, the jam will set better.
— The bars can be stored in an airtight container in the cupboard for up to three days and in the refrigerator for a week. Or freeze and defrost the day before enjoying.

Ultimate Porridge

SERVES 2
—
PREP TIME 5 MINS
COOK TIME 15 MINUTES

Porridge is by far my favourite, and most eaten, breakfast. It is a staple in a vegan diet as it is simple, healthy and easy to adapt throughout the seasons. It may seem like a basic recipe, but having patience is key to making it go from an average bowl of oats to a hug in a bowl. Ensure you don't overcook or overheat the oats by starting with a ratio of 1:3 oats to liquid and cook over a medium heat. (If you want a quicker breakfast, opt for less chunky oats and do a 1:2 oats to liquid ratio.)

100 g (3½ oz/1 cup) rolled oats
750 ml (25 fl oz/3 cups) boiling
  water
pinch of salt
splash of non-dairy milk (my
  favourite is oat or coconut)
½ teaspoon ground cinnamon
maple syrup or brown sugar,
  for the topping
fruits, nuts, nut butters, seeds or
  treats you like, to serve

1. Add the oats and boiling water to a high-edged saucepan over a medium heat. Bring to an almost boil, then reduce the heat to a simmer, add the salt and keep stirring. Be sure not to overheat or overcook the porridge. The key is not to rush it, but instead keep stirring as it simmers away, taking the time to let it cook to the perfect creamy consistency. I find after 10–15 minutes, it is perfect.
2. Just before the porridge is your ideal consistency, stir through a splash of non-dairy milk and the cinnamon, then remove the pan from the heat. You can now stir in the chia seeds, if using.
3. Pour into a bowl, then drizzle with maple syrup or a sprinkling of brown sugar. Allow the sugars to melt into the porridge and finish with whatever fruits, nuts, nut butters, seeds or treats you like.

IDEAS FOR TOPPINGS:
— Create a berry compote by heating a mug of frozen berries in a large saucepan with a splash of water and 1 teaspoon of brown sugar, simmering over a medium heat for 10–15 minutes until caramelised.
— Add orange slices, vegan dark chocolate chunks and pistachios.
— Add sliced mango, kiwi and coconut sugar.

Maple Pancakes

MAKES 4-6
—
PREP TIME 15 MINS
COOK TIME 10-15 MINS

There are hundreds of different ways to make pancakes, but this recipe is probably my favourite for texture and taste. Not too flat, too fluffy, too sweet or too bland (I've tried many a bland vegan pancake). This version uses apple cider vinegar as a substitute to create the 'buttermilk', and is my go-to any time I'm craving pancakes. Adding maple syrup to the batter makes it extra rich in flavour, but it can be left out, if you prefer. Feel free to throw some chocolate chips or blueberries into the batter too.

---

125 g (4½ oz/1 cup) self-raising (self-rising) flour (or gluten-free flour)
½ teaspoon ground cinnamon
2 tablespoons caster (superfine) sugar
pinch of sea salt
240 ml (8 fl oz/scant 1 cup) non-dairy milk
1 tablespoon apple cider vinegar
2 tablespoons maple syrup
1 teaspoon vanilla extract
2 teaspoons olive oil or use a spray oil
handful of fresh berries, to serve

1. Sift the flour into a large bowl with the cinnamon, sugar and salt and stir together with a wooden spoon.
2. In a separate measuring jug, pour in the milk, apple cider vinegar, maple syrup and vanilla extract and stir together. Leave to stand for 10 minutes.
3. Combine the wet mixture with the dry mixture and whisk until mixed, making sure not to overmix (it's fine if there are a few lumps).
4. Heat a non-stick frying pan over a medium heat with a small drizzle of oil (I like to use a spray oil). Add a ladleful of the pancake mix to the pan, about 120 ml (4 fl oz/½ cup) per pancake, and cook until the pancake starts to come up around the edges, about 5–7 minutes. Have a little peak underneath to see if it's golden, then flip over and cook for another 5–7 minutes, or until brown. Transfer to a plate (I put the cooked pancakes in a low oven to keep warm) and repeat the process until all the mixture is used up.
5. Serve with an extra drizzle of maple syrup, some fresh berries and whatever other toppings you fancy.

TIP
— Make your own berry compote to pour on top (see my Berry Chia Jam recipe on page 47), which can be made ahead of time and stored in a sterilised jar for up to two weeks, or in the freezer.

MAKE IT VEGAN

Marmalady Muffins

MAKES 12
—
PREP TIME 10 MINS
COOK TIME 20 MINS

A muffin in the morning is always a good idea, and these are made with zesty marmalade and orange juice, then spiced with cinnamon! The bitterness from the marmalade mixed with the sweetness of the brown sugar and the spice of the cinnamon is a match made in muffin heaven. Vegan baking can be incredibly easy with just a few switches and you wouldn't taste the difference!

120 ml (4 fl oz/½ cup) vegetable oil, plus extra to grease
225 g (8 oz/1¾ cups) plain (all-purpose) flour
75 g (2½ oz/scant ½ cup) brown sugar
2 teaspoons baking powder
pinch of bicarbonate of soda (baking soda)
1 teaspoon ground cinnamon
pinch of salt
grated zest of 1 orange
225 ml (7½ fl oz/scant 1 cup) orange juice
2 tablespoons marmalade

1. Preheat a fan oven to 180°C (400°F) and grease a 12-hole muffin tin (pan).
2. Add the flour, sugar, baking powder, bicarbonate of soda, cinnamon, salt and orange zest to a large bowl and mix until well combined.
3. In another bowl, stir the orange juice together with the vegetable oil and marmalade.
4. Combine the wet and dry ingredients and stir well. Don't worry about lumps as long as the flour is incorporated. Pour the mixture into the muffin tin (roughly 2 tablespoons per muffin).
5. Bake in the oven for about 20 minutes, or until golden brown. Leave to cool for 5 minutes, then enjoy.

TIP
— For a subtler orange taste, omit the orange zest.

Plant-based Pains au Chocolat

It's surprisingly easy to make your own pains au chocolat at home – and make them vegan (fortunately, most brands of ready-made puff pastry are vegan)! Like many of my recipes, the inspiration comes from my childhood when my mum would make the instant versions from a tin that would pop open and reveal the pastry inside. We'd roll them out, add the chocolate to the middle and enjoy straight from the oven.

MAKES 6
—
PREP TIME 10-15 MINS
COOK TIME 20-25 MINS

plain (all-purpose) flour, for dusting
350 g (12 oz) sheet of vegan puff pastry
about 50 g (1¾ oz) vegan dark chocolate with at least 70% cocoa solids
non-dairy milk, for brushing
icing (powdered) sugar, for dusting

1. Preheat a fan oven to 180°C (400°F). Line a large baking tray (pan) with a silicone sheet or baking parchment.
2. Sprinkle a light layer of flour onto the work surface, cut the pastry sheet in half, then cut each half into three, making six strips.
3. Roughly chop the chocolate into rectangular strips (don't worry if it falls apart a bit). Sprinkle the chocolate in a line (to replicate a chocolate baton) at the top end of each strip of pastry. Roll the pastry over the chocolate, then add another line of chocolate along the crease where the pastry meets, then roll all the way to the end.
4. Brush the pastry with non-dairy milk and arrange the pains au chocolat on the prepared baking tray.
5. Bake for 20–25 minutes until golden, then remove from the oven and sift some icing sugar on top to decorate. Wait for 5 minutes to cool slightly and enjoy.

TIP
— Once you've created your pains au chocolat, freeze them before baking, then cook from frozen later

WAKE UP

56–87

Quick

Eats

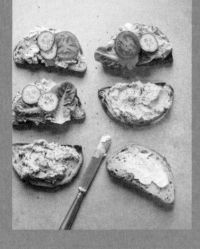

Chickpea 'Tuna' Sandwich p. 83

Pizza Toast p. 80

Spinach and Butter Bean Soup p. 64

15-minute Stir-fry Noodles p. 66

Protein Pepper Pasta p. 84

Oyster Mushroom Salad p. 63

Smoky Quesadillas p. 72

Everything Bowls p. 74

Mediterranean Vegetable Turnovers p. 69

10-minute Mac 'n' Cheese p. 87

Sesame, Ginger and
Mint Noodle Salad p. 60

Tom Yum Soup p. 70

Sesame, Ginger and Mint Noodle Salad

Sesame oil's delicious nutty aroma makes me want to drizzle it over every noodle dish I prepare! My husband, Alex, always requests this noodle salad, and I think it's great for those who aren't huge vegetable fans. The dressing is so more-ish that I love to pour it over many different dishes. You can even substitute the tahini for peanut butter for a satay flavour, or leave it out entirely (along with the water) if you aren't keen.

SERVES 2-3
—
PREP TIME 10 MINS
COOK TIME 10 MINS

150–200 g (5½–7 oz) soba
  or udon noodles
¼ red cabbage
1 carrot
1 cucumber
2 spring onions (scallions), sliced
sprig of mint, chopped
handful of coriander (cilantro),
  chopped
2 tablespoons sesame seeds

FOR THE DRESSING
3 tablespoons hulled tahini
  (see tip on page 105)
2 tablespoons water
1 tablespoon soy sauce
  (or tamari for a gluten-free
  option)
1 teaspoon maple syrup
2 teaspoons toasted sesame oil
thumb-sized piece (about
  5 cm/2 in) of fresh ginger root,
  finely chopped or minced
1 garlic clove, finely chopped
grated zest and juice of 1 lime
pinch of chilli (hot pepper) flakes

1. Cook the noodles in a large saucepan of boiling water for 8–10 minutes, then drain and rinse under cold running water. Set aside.
2. Meanwhile, thinly slice the cabbage and create ribbons with the carrot and cucumber with a vegetable peeler (or use a grater if you're feeling lazy). Add all the vegetables, herbs and sesame seeds to a large salad bowl with the noodles and mix together.
3. Whisk all the dressing ingredients together in a small bowl. Drizzle over the salad ingredients and stir to combine. Serve cold straightaway or leave in the refrigerator for up to five days.

TIP
— If you don't need all the dressing, store in an airtight container in the refrigerator for up to a week to use again.

MAKE IT VEGAN

Oyster Mushroom Salad

SERVES 2
—
PREP TIME 5 MINS
COOK TIME 5 MINS

I could eat fresh authentic Thai food every day, after getting a taste for all the delicious flavours during my six-week stay in Thailand a few years ago. Luckily, there's a restaurant local to us in St Ives, in Cornwall, that makes the most delicious Thai food, which takes me right back to my holiday. My favourite dish is their oyster mushroom salad, which I immediately had to cook after trying it for the first time. The star of the show, of course, is the meaty and flavourful oyster mushrooms (my absolute favourite) which soak up the delicious mix of flavours.

2–3 king oyster mushrooms, shredded
4 garlic cloves, sliced
thumb-sized piece (about 5 cm/2 in) of fresh ginger root, sliced into matchsticks
2 spring onions (scallions), green and white parts separated and chopped
1½ teaspoons sugar (brown or coconut)
salt and freshly ground black pepper
3 tablespoons vegetable oil
1 red chilli, chopped (remove the seeds if you prefer less spice)
grated zest and juice of 1 lime
3 tablespoons light soy sauce (or tamari for a gluten-free option)
1 teaspoon toasted sesame oil
1 tablespoon sesame seeds
handful of chopped coriander (cilantro)

1. Blanch the shredded oyster mushrooms in a pan of boiling water for 1–2 minutes, then drain.
2. Add the drained mushrooms to a large serving bowl and top with the sliced garlic, ginger, white part of the spring onion and sugar and season to taste with salt and pepper.
3. Heat the oil in a small frying pan, add the chilli and fry for 2 minutes to infuse. Throw in the lime zest, then remove the pan from the heat.
4. Drizzle the oil mixture on top of all the ingredients in the bowl and carefully stir everything together (it will smell delicious).
5. Pour over the soy sauce, lime juice, sesame oil, sesame seeds and mix together. Top with the green parts of the spring onion and chopped coriander and serve.

TIPS
— This recipe also works well with other fast-cooking vegetables like broccoli, spinach, pak choi (bok choi), cabbage, carrot or kale.
— Tofu would be a delicious addition if you're looking to increase the amount of protein or to make this dish more of a main meal.

Spinach and Butter Bean Soup

This hearty soup is the perfect meal on a cold day, or when you're in need of something comforting. Creamy beans paired with colourful spinach are a wholesome combination. Packed with protein, fibre and iron, this soup is also extra nutritious. Plus, it's super flexible, as you can swap the butter (lima) beans for cannellini, borlotti (cranberry) or chickpeas (garbanzos), add a tin of tinned tomatoes and tomato purée (paste) with a teaspoon of smoked paprika, or zing it up with a splash of Tabasco.

SERVES 4

—

PREP TIME 5 MINS
COOK TIME 15 MINS

2 tablespoons olive oil
1 large onion, finely chopped
1 leek, finely chopped
2 celery stalks, finely chopped
2 garlic cloves, grated
handful of thyme, leaves picked
2 × 400 g (14 oz) tins of butter (lima) beans, drained and rinsed
250 g (9 oz) young spinach or use frozen
2 tablespoons nutritional yeast
grated zest and juice of 1 lemon
1.2 litres (40 fl oz/5 cups) vegetable stock
salt and freshly ground black pepper
warm crusty bread, to serve

OPTIONAL
pinch of chilli (hot pepper) flakes or splash of Tabasco sauce, to serve

1. Heat the olive oil in a large saucepan, add the chopped onion, leek and celery and cook over a medium heat for 5–10 minutes until softened. Add the garlic and thyme leaves and cook for another minute.
2. Add the butter beans to the pan along with the spinach, nutritional yeast, lemon juice and zest, and vegetable stock, then season to taste. Bring to the boil, then remove the pan from the heat.
3. Serve sprinkled with red chilli flakes or Tabasco sauce (if using) and enjoy with warm crusty bread.

QUICK EATS

15-minute Stir-fry Noodles

We make a stir-fry every week without fail. Mainly because it's so quick and easy. Plus, it can be thrown together with whatever ingredients you have in the refrigerator, making it ideal if you need to use some vegetables, or haven't been shopping recently. It can be as simple as you like, and adapted in so many ways to match what you have to hand, or what you're craving that day. I've added some lazy and time-friendly hacks to make this recipe even simpler.

SERVES 2
—
PREP TIME 10 MINS
COOK TIME 15–20 MINS

400g (14 oz) block
   of extra-firm tofu
200 g (7 oz) mushrooms (any
   work, but my favourite are
   chestnut, shiitake, oyster or
   Portobello)
300 g (10½ oz) kale, broccoli,
   pak choi (bok choi) or cabbage
1 red chilli
3 garlic cloves
thumb-sized piece (about
   5 cm/2 in) of fresh ginger root
2 bunches of noodles (my
   favourite are udon or soba
   for a gluten-free option)
1 tablespoon olive or coconut oil
1 tablespoon maple syrup or use
   agave syrup, brown sugar or
   other sweetener
1 tablespoon dark soy sauce (or
   tamari for a gluten-free option)
1 tablespoon light soy sauce (or
   tamari for a gluten-free option)
grated zest and juice of 1 lemon
   or lime

OPTIONAL
sesame seeds, to serve
toasted sesame oil, to serve
handful of chopped coriander
   (cilantro) leaves, to serve

1. Cube the tofu into bite-sized chunks, chop all the veg, finely chop the chilli and mince the garlic and ginger. I use a garlic press to mince garlic straight into the pan to make it extra quick.
2. Put the noodles in a saucepan of boiling water to cook, bring back to a boil and reduce to a simmer (about 5–8 minutes depending on the noodles). When the noodles are ready, set aside a ladleful of noodle water, then rinse the noodles under cold running water.
3. Meanwhile, in a large frying pan or wok, add the oil, garlic, ginger and chilli and fry over a high heat for a couple of minutes (adding the oil and garlic at the same time stops it from burning as easily).
4. Then add the tofu and vegetables and fry for another 5 minutes. Now everything's cooked, pour in the maple syrup (or sweetener of your choice), soy sauces, lemon or lime zest and juice, and stir together.
5. Add the noodles to the pan, along with the reserved noodle water and toss everything together. Serve with an optional topping of sesame seeds, a drizzle of sesame oil and a sprinkling of coriander.

TIP
— If you have time, I would recommend pressing the tofu in a tofu press (which can be bought online) or between a dish towel and two plates topped with some heavy cookbooks to remove excess moisture, chopping into bite-sized cubes, then frying in a large pan for 10 minutes until browned. I regularly skip this step because I just want to eat everything immediately, but it does make a difference if you like your tofu to be extra golden and have a crisp exterior.

QUICK EATS

MAKE IT VEGAN

Mediterranean Vegetable Turnovers

A savoury golden crusted pastry filled with fresh vegetables that's simple and hearty, this dish is also totally adaptable for the vegetables you have to hand or are in season. I've used red onions, fresh spinach, red (bell) peppers, potato and sweetcorn, with vegan pesto, paprika and lemon for an ultra-flavourful filling. If using a different combination of vegetables, just make sure that you cook those with a particularly high water content (courgette/zucchini, aubergine/eggplant, tomato, mushrooms) first to reduce the liquid content. You can also make a sweet turnover with apple, cinnamon and brown sugar, or vegan chocolate spread and berries!

MAKES 4
—
PREP TIME 15-20 MINS
COOK TIME 25-30 MINS

200 g (7 oz) baby spinach
1 tablespoon olive oil
1 red onion, thinly sliced
1 red (bell) pepper, chopped
½ tin (130 g/4½ oz) drained
   sweetcorn
2 teaspoons paprika
grated zest of 1 lemon
dash of Tabasco sauce
salt and freshly ground black
   pepper
320 g (11 oz) sheet of ready-
   rolled vegan puff pastry
   (Jus-Rol is vegan)
190 g (7 oz) jar vegan pesto
1 white potato, thinly sliced
1 tablespoon non-dairy milk,
   for glazing
dressed mixed salad, to serve

OPTIONAL
handful of grated vegan cheese

1. Preheat a fan oven to 220°C (475°F). Wilt the spinach in a saucepan of boiling water for a minute or two, and pat dry.
2. Heat the olive oil in a frying pan, add the onion and pepper and fry over a medium heat for 5 minutes. Next, add the spinach, sweetcorn, paprika, lemon zest and Tabasco sauce and cook until any water has evaporated. Season with salt and pepper.
3. Cut the sheet of pastry into four pieces. Spread the pesto all over each piece, leaving a 1 cm (½ in) border. Arrange the potato slices neatly to cover half of each piece, leaving a 2 cm (¾ in) border all around the pastry.
4. Arrange the cooked vegetables on top of the potato, then add the grated cheese (if using). Brush the border with milk, then bring one corner over to the opposite corner, seal using your fingers and crimp the edges with a fork.
5. Brush the top with a little more milk and cut three diagonal slits in each of the pastry turnovers.
6. Bake in the oven for 25–30 minutes until the pastry is golden brown and puffed up. Serve with a dressed mixed salad.

TIP
— Once you've assembled the pastries, pop them in the freezer to pull out as and when you need them, then simply bake in the oven. Since they're frozen, add 10–15 minutes extra to the cooking time. You can also bake them first (reducing the cooking time by 5 minutes), then put them in the freezer once they're cooled and simply reheat in the oven for the final 5 minutes when you want to enjoy!

Tom Yum Soup

This is another dish inspired by my visit to Thailand. I had tom yum soup basically every day I was there. I just couldn't get enough of the perfect blend of spicy and sour flavours from the lemongrass, lime leaves, galangal and chilli. The distinct citrusy flavour mixed with a spicy kick from the chilli is truly a match made in heaven. Typically, the dish includes fish sauce and is made with prawns (shrimp), but a vegetarian option omits the fish sauce (I replaced this savoury flavour with soy sauce) and uses vegetables instead. Enjoy with a side of rice or throw in some tofu for a satisfying meal.

SERVES 2
—
PREP TIME 5-10 MINS
COOK TIME 10 MINS

2 lemongrass stalks
8 slices of galangal or use galangal paste if you can't find fresh
6 makrut lime leaves
2–4 red or bird's eye chillies
4 garlic cloves
200 g (7 oz) mushrooms (oyster, king oyster, shiitake, enoki or chestnut are the best)
100 g (3½ oz) cherry tomatoes
1 litre (34 fl oz/4¼ cups) vegetable stock
1 tablespoon brown or coconut sugar
3 tablespoons soy sauce (or tamari for a gluten-free option)
juice of 3–5 limes

TO SERVE
handful of coriander (cilantro) leaves
jasmine rice

1. Prepare the ingredients by trimming the ends of the lemongrass, smashing with the back of a knife and chopping into 7.5 cm (3 in) lengths, then slicing in half. Slice the galangal. Tear the lime leaves. Smash the chillies and cut into big chunks, then mince the garlic. Slice the mushrooms and halve the tomatoes.
2. Add the vegetable stock, lemongrass, galangal, lime leaves, chillies and garlic to a medium saucepan. Bring to the boil, then reduce the heat and simmer for 5 minutes.
3. Add the mushrooms with the cherry tomatoes, sugar and soy sauce and return to the boil. Reduce to a simmer and cook for a minute or two, remove from the heat and add the lime juice.
4. Serve topped with coriander and with a side of jasmine rice.

TIPS
— The lemongrass, makrut lime leaves and galangal are tough, so aren't intended to be eaten. They instead infuse the soup with delicious flavour, so you can remove them before adding the mushrooms, etc., if you prefer.
— If you want a creamier soup, similar to a tom kha, reduce the stock to 500 ml (17 fl oz/generous 2 cups) and add a 400 ml (14 fl oz) tin of coconut milk along with the mushrooms and cherry tomatoes.

Smoky Quesadillas

SERVES 2
—
PREP TIME 5 MINS
COOK TIME 5-10 MINS

I love a quesadilla for lunch or an end-of-the-week dinner. You can fill them with absolutely anything you want, or just stick to simple vegan cheese! I like to add some smoked paprika and chilli (hot pepper) flakes for an extra kick, and accompany them with a squeeze of fresh lime juice, salsa and guacamole.

1 teaspoon olive oil
2 flour (or corn for gluten-free) tortillas
100 g (3½ oz) vegan cheese, grated
1 spring onion (scallion), thinly sliced
handful of cherry tomatoes, finely chopped
¼ tin (60 g/2 oz) black, kidney or pinto beans, drained and rinsed
½ teaspoon smoked paprika
½ teaspoon chilli (hot pepper) flakes
salt and freshly ground black pepper

TO SERVE
fresh lime juice
Quick Guacamole (page 125), Salsa (page 125)

1. Heat a non-stick frying pan over a medium to high heat with a little oil swirled around the pan for a minute or two, before adding the first tortilla. Flip the tortilla over a couple of times for a few minutes, until air pockets form.

2. Sprinkle a handful of grated vegan cheese over the tortilla, then top with your chosen ingredients. My favourite is thinly sliced spring onions, chopped tomatoes and black beans. Make sure you don't overfill the tortilla!

3. Sprinkle with a small pinch of paprika and chilli flakes, then season with salt and pepper. Cook for around 3–5 minutes, or until the cheese is melted.

4. Carefully flip over one side of the tortilla with a spatula (like an omelette), pressing down lightly. The bottom side should be golden brown in colour. Set the first quesadilla aside and repeat for the second tortilla.

5. Transfer to a cutting board, cut into quarters, squeeze some lime juice over the top and serve straightaway with a side of guacamole and salsa.

TIP
— Add the mushroom walnut 'meat' (page 124) for an extra meaty taste.

Everything Bowls

A big bowl of goodness is my most commonly eaten lunch. The formula for this is a balanced bowl of carbs, fats and protein that can be changed up day to day and week to week. For each recipe I have shared a theme for the ingredients, but I mix and match these all the time, usually following no recipe at all. All you need is a base of a grain (rice, quinoa, couscous, pasta, burghul, pearl barley ...), accompanied by a source of protein (tofu, chickpeas/garbanzos, kidney beans, butter/lima beans, lentils, vegan meat alternatives ...), vegetables or salad (lettuce, rocket/arugula, cucumber, carrots, mushrooms, kale, spinach, bell/sweet peppers, tomatoes ...), healthy fats (avocado, olive oil, nuts, seeds, vegan cheese, hummus ...) and some flavour or dressing (sriracha, lime or lemon juice, vinegar, soy sauce ...). Get creative!

Green Bowl

● GLUTEN-FREE   ● SOY-FREE

SERVES 2

—

PREP TIME 10 MINS
COOK TIME 40 MINS

½ (or 1 small) head of broccoli, chopped
100 g (3½ oz) curly kale or cavolo nero, chopped
3 garlic cloves, left whole
olive oil, for drizzling
salt and freshly ground black pepper
100 g (3½ oz/½ cup) quinoa
250 ml (8 fl oz/1 cup) water
½ vegetable stock cube
grated zest and juice of ½ lemon
60 g (2 oz) rocket (arugula)
½ cucumber, grated
200 g (7 oz) edamame beans (out of the pods)
1 spring onion (scallion), finely chopped
approx. 1 tablespoon seed mix (sunflower, pumpkin), for sprinkling
1 tablespoon Easy Vegan Pesto (page 108)

For when you need some green goodness in your life. Refreshing, full of fibre and, you guessed it, greens.

1. Preheat a fan oven to 200°C (425°F).
2. Add the broccoli, kale or cavelo nero, and whole garlic cloves to a large roasting tin. Drizzle with olive oil and season with salt and pepper. Roast in the oven for 15–20 minutes, turning the vegetables halfway through cooking.
3. Meanwhile, rinse the quinoa in a colander. Add to a medium saucepan with the measured water and stock cube, bring to the boil, stir to mix in the stock cube, then reduce the heat and simmer for 10–15 minutes until the water has been absorbed. Remove from the heat, cover with a lid and leave to steam for 5 minutes. Stir through the lemon zest, then fluff with a fork.
4. To assemble the bowls, start with a bed of rocket, then top with the quinoa, broccoli, kale or cavolo nero, and garlic mix, and the cucumber. Sprinkle over the edamame beans, a squeeze of lemon juice, spring onion, seeds and a drizzle of pesto.

Sushi bowl

● GLUTEN-FREE OPTION   ● NUT-FREE

SERVES 2

—

PREP TIME 15 MINS
COOK TIME 35 MINS

1½ blocks of tofu
220 g (7½ oz/1 cup) sushi rice
250 ml (8 fl oz/1 cup) water
1 tablespoon rice vinegar
drizzle of olive oil
1 tablespoon soy sauce
  (or tamari for a gluten-free
  option)
1 teaspoon sriracha
½ cucumber, chopped
1 carrot, grated
1 avocado, peeled, stoned
  and sliced
2 sheets of nori, thinly sliced
  or kept in pieces (I like to keep
  in pieces to scoop up the
  sushi bowl toppings)
sesame seeds, for sprinkling
salt and freshly ground
  black pepper

FOR THE DRESSING
2 tablespoons soy sauce
  (or tamari for a gluten-free
  option)
2 teaspoons toasted sesame oil
2 teaspoons maple syrup
juice of 1 lime
1 cm (½ in) piece of fresh
  ginger root, grated

OPTIONAL TOPPINGS
kimchi
sriracha mayonnaise
wasabi
sushi ginger

A sushi bowl makes the process of making sushi that little bit simpler, while getting the delicious flavours from the sushi we know and love.

1. Press the tofu (see tip on page 66) and set aside.
2. Rinse the rice in a saucepan until the water runs clear, filling up with water, swirling around with your fingers and then draining the milky water. Repeat two to three times. Drain the rice in a sieve (fine mesh strainer) and return to the saucepan. Pour in the measured water and leave to soak for up to 30 minutes (if you don't have time, you can skip this step). Cook the rice by bringing it to the boil, then reducing the heat to low, covering with a lid and simmering for 10 minutes. Turn off the heat and steam for another 10 minutes. Finally, pour over the rice vinegar, and using a spatula, slice and fold through, being careful not to overmix or turn the rice mushy. Leave to cool.
3. Meanwhile, chop the tofu into cubes and fry in a medium frying pan with a little oil over a medium to high heat for 10–15 minutes, or until golden brown. When golden, drizzle in a little soy sauce and sriracha for flavour and season with salt and pepper.
4. Mix all the dressing ingredients together in a small bowl and set aside.
5. To assemble the bowls, start with the sushi rice and tofu, then add the cucumber, carrot, avocado and nori. Top with a sprinkle of sesame seeds and pour over the dressing. I also love to serve with some kimchi, sriracha mayo, wasabi and sushi ginger on top.

TIP
— If short on time, use instant, basmati or long-grain rice (I often do this if making for lunch).

Burrito Bowl

● GLUTEN-FREE   ● NUT-FREE   ● SOY-FREE

SERVES 2
—
PREP TIME 10 MINS
COOK TIME 55 MINS

100 g (3½ oz/½ cup) brown rice
250 ml (8 fl oz/1 cup) water
½ teaspoon sea salt
Salsa (page 125) or use shop-
  bought or chopped tomatoes
Quick Guacamole (page 125) or
  just use mashed avocado
½ tin (120 g/4 oz) black or kidney
  beans, drained and rinsed
150–200 g (5½–7 oz) sweetcorn,
  drained and rinsed
1 red (bell) pepper, sliced
½ head of crisp lettuce, sliced
juice of ½ lime
handful of coriander (cilantro)
  leaves

OPTIONAL EXTRAS
100–150g (3½–5½ oz) vegan
  chicken

Similar to my sushi bowl, deconstruct your burrito into a bowl of
Mexican-inspired goodness.

1. Rinse the brown rice in a sieve (fine mesh strainer). Add to a large
   saucepan with the measured water and salt and bring to the boil.
   Reduce the heat to a simmer, cover with a lid and cook for 30
   minutes. Turn off the heat and leave to steam for 10 minutes. Fluff
   with a fork.
2. Meanwhile, prepare the salsa and guacamole following the
   instructions on page 125. Fry the vegan chicken (if using) in a frying
   pan with a little hot sauce over a medium to high heat for 10 minutes
   until golden brown.
3. To assemble the bowls, add the rice, then layer up the beans,
   sweetcorn, pepper, lettuce, and vegan chicken (if using). Squeeze
   over the lime juice and sprinkle on extra coriander.

Mediterranean Bowl

SERVES 2

—

PREP TIME 10 MINS
COOK TIME 30 MINS

200 g (7 oz/1 cup) couscous
200 ml (7 fl oz/scant 1 cup)
   boiling water with 1 vegetable
   stock cube
olive oil, for drizzling
100 g (3½ oz) baby spinach
½ tin (120 g/4 oz) of chickpeas
   (garbanzos), drained and
   rinsed
½ cucumber, chopped
200 g (7 oz) cherry tomatoes
   or use sundried tomatoes,
   chopped
½ red onion, chopped
handful of olives, pitted and
   chopped
about 100 g (3½ oz) hummus
pinch of chilli (hot pepper) flakes
juice of ½ lemon
handful of parsley, chopped
handful of vegan Feta (see
   No-feta Greek Inspired Salad,
   page 150), chopped

● NUT-FREE   ● SOY-FREE

One of the healthiest diets on the planet is that enjoyed by
Mediterranean countries. We can learn a lot from them, especially
as they love their veg!

1. Add the couscous and vegetable stock to a large heatproof bowl,
   cover with a lid or plate and leave to stand for 5–10 minutes. When
   the couscous is soft, fluff it up with a fork, then drizzle with a little
   olive oil.
2. To assemble the bowls, add the spinach followed by the couscous,
   chickpeas, cucumber, tomatoes, red onion, olives and a large dollop
   of hummus on top. Sprinkle with chilli flakes, a squeeze of lemon
   juice, the parsley and some vegan feta.

Burrito Bowl

Green Bowl

MAKE IT VEGAN

Mediterranean
Bowl

Sushi Bowl

Pizza Toast

This recipe hits the spot when you're craving a pizza, but don't have one in the freezer! An ideal five-minute snack or quick lunch that doesn't involve much cooking!

SERVES 1

—

PREP TIME 5 MINS
COOK TIME 5 MINS

2 slices of bread
vegan butter or spread,
  for spreading
1–2 tablespoons tomato purée
  (paste)
salt and freshly ground black
  pepper
1 teaspoon mixed herbs (dried
  oregano, basil, thyme, sage,
  etc.)
25–50 g (1–1¾ oz) vegan cheese,
  grated
extra pizza toppings you enjoy
  (chopped olives, chopped
  red onion, sliced sweet/bell
  peppers, sliced mushrooms,
  vegan meat alternative, etc.)
olive oil, for drizzling

1. On each slice of bread, spread a layer of vegan butter. Turn over each slice and spread over a thin layer of tomato purée. Season generously with salt and pepper, then add a large sprinkle of mixed herbs.

2. On one slice, add the grated vegan cheese and, if you like, some of your favourite toppings, such as chopped olives, red onion, peppers, mushrooms and vegan meat, etc.

3. Drizzle with olive oil and close the sandwich together with the other slice of bread.

4. If using a toastie machine, place the sandwich inside and toast until golden. If using a frying pan, drizzle a little olive oil into the pan and fry on each side over a medium to high heat for 3–5 minutes, or until golden and the cheese has melted.

TIP

— Some of my favourite vegan cheeses to use for ultimate melting power are Applewood Smoky Cheese Alternative and Violife Epic Mature.

MAKE IT VEGAN

Chickpea 'Tuna' Sandwich

SERVES 4

—

PREP TIME 5 MINS

Who knew that tuna could be made from chickpeas (garbanzos)? Not quite, but it mimics the effect! A perfect sandwich filling or to top a jacket potato or crunchy green salad. The nori adds the taste of the sea, the capers a saltiness and the vinegar that nostalgic flavour.

400 g (14 oz) tin of
  chickpeas (garbanzos),
  drained and rinsed
2 tablespoons shop-bought
  vegan mayonnaise or use
  olive oil, plus extra to serve
juice of ½ lemon
1 tablespoon malt vinegar
½ red onion, roughly chopped
½ teaspoon garlic powder
1 tablespoon capers
1 sheet of nori, roughly torn
salt and freshly ground
  black pepper
bread, wrap or pitta (or
  a gluten-free option)

TO SERVE
cucumber, sliced
tomato, sliced
crunchy lettuce

1. Blend all the ingredients together in a food processor, leaving some lumps in there for texture. Taste and adjust the seasoning if needed.
2. Spread in a sandwich (or wrap, or pitta, or just go ahead and eat by itself on a spoon), and top with a classic mix of sliced cucumber, sliced tomato and some crunchy lettuce. Top with some more mayonnaise and enjoy! Use as you need and store in the refrigerator in an airtight container for up to three days.

Protein Pepper Pasta

SERVES 4
—

PREP TIME 5 MINS
COOK TIME 25–30 MINS

One of the worries for people on a vegan diet is getting enough protein. While there are many ways we can get protein from a plant-based diet, one of my favourites is working tofu and beans into recipes. Silken tofu and butter (lima) beans are deliciously creamy, working perfectly for a pasta recipe. The roasted red (bell) peppers make it super simple too!

350–400 g (12–14 oz) pasta (you can opt for high-protein legume pasta for additional protein, and to make it gluten-free, if you like)
2 tablespoons olive oil
1 onion, roughly chopped
2 garlic cloves, minced, or use 1 teaspoon garlic powder
450 g (1 lb) roasted red (bell) peppers (you can buy these in jars), drained and roughly chopped
½ tin (200 g/7 oz) butter (lima) beans, drained and rinsed
½ teaspoon chilli (hot pepper) flakes
1 teaspoon dried oregano
100 ml (3½ fl oz/scant ½ cup) vegetable stock
grated zest and juice of ½ lemon
350 g (12 oz) packet of silken tofu

OPTIONAL
nutritional yeast or vegan cheese, for sprinkling on top

1. Bring a large saucepan of salted water to the boil for the pasta. Once boiling, add the pasta and stir. Reduce the heat to a simmer for 8–10 minutes and cook the pasta until al dente, or according to the packet instructions.
2. Meanwhile, add the oil to another large pan over a medium heat, throw in the chopped onion and gently fry for 5–10 minutes, or until softened. Add the garlic and cook for a minute or two.
3. Add the chopped peppers, butter beans, chilli flakes, oregano and vegetable stock. Bring to a simmer, heating through for around 5 minutes.
4. Add the lemon zest and juice, then transfer the sauce to a blender with the silken tofu and blitz until smooth. Alternatively, use a hand-held blender. Return the sauce to the pan.
5. Once the pasta is ready, drain, saving a ladleful of the pasta water. Add the pasta and pasta water to the sauce and mix through. The pasta is perfect as it is, or with a yummy sprinkle of nutritional yeast or vegan cheese.

TIPS
— Once the sauce is blitzed, you can add any leftover vegetables that you may have in the refrigerator.
— Swap the tofu for coconut cream for a different flavour.

MAKE IT VEGAN

10-minute Mac 'n' Cheese

This is hands down the most repeated recipe in our household. I created this recipe back in 2017 after a few years of trying so many vegan mac 'n' cheese recipes that just didn't hit the spot. Most of them involved boiling some butternut squash or carrot (not what I am really after if I'm craving mac 'n' cheese) or had a lengthier method and required a lot of substitutes. This recipe only takes 10 minutes, uses ingredients you're likely to already have in your cupboard and is still my favourite to this day.

SERVES 4

—

PREP TIME 10 MINS
COOK TIME 10 MINS

500 g (1 lb 2 oz) macaroni
   (or gluten-free pasta)
grated vegan cheese or green
   vegetables of choice, to serve
   (optional)

**FOR THE CASHEW
   CHEESE SAUCE**
80 g (2¾ oz/½ cup) cashews
45 g (1½ oz/1 cup) nutritional
   yeast
250 ml (8 fl oz/1 cup) non-dairy
   milk
250 ml (8 fl oz/1 cup) water
3 tablespoons cornflour
   (cornstarch)
juice of 1 lemon
1 teaspoon salt
1 teaspoon garlic powder
1 teaspoon onion powder
1 teaspoon mustard powder
½ teaspoon paprika
½ teaspoon ground turmeric
pinch of chilli powder
freshly ground black pepper

1. Cook the macaroni in a large saucepan of boiling water for 8–10 minutes until al dente, or according to the packet instructions.
2. Meanwhile, blitz all the sauce ingredients together in a blender until smooth (give this time as the cashews need to break down). Taste and adjust the seasoning, if needed.
3. Once the pasta is cooked, drain and return it to the pan. Stir the cheese sauce into the pasta over a low heat, stirring it constantly until the sauce thickens.
4. Serve the mac 'n' cheese by itself, grate over some vegan cheese, or enjoy with a side of green vegetables.

TIP
— If you don't have a high-speed blender, soak the cashews in boiling water for 1 hour prior to starting the recipe, to help them to blend.

88–125

Main

Event

Sundried Tomato and Tahini Rigatoni p. 105

Butter No-chicken Curry p. 100

Homemade Pizza p. 99

Sticky Seitan Ribs p. 110

Parmigiana Melanzane p. 95

Pasta alla Norma p. 92

Kao Soi p. 106

Garlic Pesto Artichoke Gnocchi p. 108

Roast Aubergine with Harissa Yoghurt p. 113

Cauliflower and Mushroom Burgers p. 118

Tofu Satay Curry p. 102

Firecracker Tofu Nuggets p. 114

Black Bean Meatballs p. 96

Beetroot Mushroom Wellington p. 122

Dirty Fries p. 124

Vegan Paella p. 121

Coconut Beetroot Risotto p. 117

Pasta alla Norma

For our honeymoon we visited the French Riviera. While we were there our beautiful hotel catered amazingly to our vegan diets, making us probably the best pasta dish I have ever eaten in my life. It helped that we were eating it looking out across the water with a glass of rosé, but that's beside the point. Pasta alla norma is an aubergine- (eggplant-) based pasta sauce that I've attempted to recreate to take me back to that blissful time.

SERVES 4
—
PREP TIME 25 MINS
COOK TIME 50 MINS

2 aubergines (eggplants), about 700 g (1 lb 9 oz), cut into 1 cm (½ in) slices
salt and freshly ground black pepper
2 tablespoons olive oil, plus extra for drizzling
4 garlic cloves, finely chopped
pinch of chilli (hot pepper) flakes (optional)
400 g (14 oz) tin of chopped tomatoes
2 tablespoons tomato purée (paste)
bunch of basil, leaves picked and stalks reserved
1 teaspoon dried mixed or Italian herbs
1 tablespoon red wine vinegar
300 g (10½ oz) rigatoni, penne or fusilli (or gluten-free pasta)

1. Line one or two large baking trays (pans) with baking parchment.
2. Arrange the aubergine slices in a single layer on the prepared baking tray(s) and sprinkle with salt. Leave to stand for 10–20 minutes to draw out the moisture. Remove the excess moisture with a paper towel or clean dish towel.
3. Meanwhile, preheat a fan oven to 200°C (425°F).
4. Drizzle the aubergine with olive oil, season with salt and pepper, and roast in the oven for 30 minutes, or until golden brown, turning the slices halfway through cooking.
5. Meanwhile, make the sauce. Add the olive oil to a large deep saucepan, then add the garlic and chilli flakes (if using) and fry over a medium heat for a few minutes, stirring constantly. Add the chopped tomatoes, then fill the empty tomato tin halfway with water, pour into the pan and add the tomato purée, basil stalks, dried herbs and vinegar. Bring to the boil, then reduce the heat and simmer until the aubergines are ready. Stir in the aubergines.
6. Bring a large saucepan of salted water to the boil, add the pasta and cook for 8–10 minutes until al dente, or according to the packet instructions. Drain the pasta, setting aside a little of the pasta water to add to the sauce to toss, then add both to the sauce.
7. Drizzle with additional olive oil, stir in the pasta and serve with the basil leaves on top.

TIP
— For a vegan version of ricotta (which is traditionally used to top this dish), use a shop-bought vegan cream cheese or Greek-style cheese and dollop on top.

MAKE IT VEGAN

Parmigiana Melanzane

SERVES 4
—
PREP TIME 15 MINS
COOK TIME 1 HOUR

This was one of the dishes prepared by our amazingly talented caterers (Dish Cornwall) on our wedding day, who made the most impressive vegan buffet spread for all our guests. We heard all day long how incredible the food was (with many saying that it was the best wedding food they'd ever had). As with so many of my other recipes, I wanted to recreate it and share it in this book because not only is it delicious, but also incredibly meaningful to me. Although I didn't eat much of it on the actual day due to nerves, at least now I can make my own version at home whenever I want to reminisce.

2 aubergines (eggplants), thinly sliced lengthways
2 courgettes (zucchini), sliced lengthways
2 tablespoons olive oil
150 g (5½ oz) vegan cheese (I use vegan mozzarella and Cheddar mixed, but vegan Parmesan is also good), grated

FOR THE TOMATO SAUCE
1 onion, finely chopped
2 garlic cloves, finely chopped
400 g (14 oz) tin of chopped tomatoes
2 tablespoons tomato purée (paste)
1 teaspoon dried oregano
few drops of Tabasco sauce or pinch of chilli (hot pepper) flakes
small bunch of basil
salt and freshly ground black pepper

FOR THE TOPPING
2 slices of brown bread, made into breadcrumbs (you can substitute with a gluten-free option) by blitzing in a blender or food processor
50 g (1¾ oz) vegan cheese, grated
1 teaspoon paprika

OPTIONAL
crusty bread, to serve
green salad, to serve

1. Heat a large frying pan over a high heat. Brush each slice of aubergine and courgette with around 1 tablespoon of olive oil and place three or four slices in the pan. Don't overcrowd the pan. Leave the slices for a couple of minutes to brown on each side, then once golden, remove and set aside on a plate. Repeat until all the slices are browned.

2. For the sauce, heat the remaining oil in the pan over a medium heat, add the onion and fry for 5–10 minutes, or until softened. Add the garlic and cook for another minute.

3. Add the chopped tomatoes, tomato purée and dried oregano. Fill the empty tomato tin halfway with water and add to the pan, then add a few drops of Tabasco sauce or some chilli flakes and season with salt and pepper. Stir and cook over a medium to low heat for about 20 minutes.

4. Meanwhile, prepare the topping by mixing all the ingredients together in a bowl. Set aside.

5. Tear the basil into the sauce, then taste and adjust the seasoning, if needed.

6. Spread about 3 tablespoons of the tomato sauce on the base of a medium gratin dish, then add a layer of the aubergines and courgettes. Sprinkle over some of the cheese and repeat until all the aubergine and courgettes have been used up, finishing with a layer of aubergine and courgettes.

7. Sprinkle the topping mixture over the aubergine and courgettes and roast in the oven for 30 minutes, or until the top is golden.

8. Serve with fresh crusty bread and a green salad.

Black Bean Meatballs

Black beans are an amazing ingredient to use when replicating any type of beef or pork recipe. Their colour and earthy taste make them one of my favourite beans to use every week. Meatballs are such a comforting meal and can be served with pasta or inside a large crusty baguette.

SERVES 4
—
PREP TIME 15-20 MINS
COOK TIME 1 HOUR

1 onion, chopped
2 garlic cloves, chopped
2 tablespoons olive oil
400 g (14 oz) tin of black beans, drained and rinsed
75 g (2½ oz/¾ cup) rolled oats
1 teaspoon harissa paste (I like spicy but reduce the amount if you prefer mild)
1 teaspoon dried oregano
1 tablespoon balsamic vinegar
100 g (3½ oz/1¼ cups) fresh breadcrumbs
sea salt and freshly ground black pepper
1 baguette
vegan cheese

FOR THE TOMATO SAUCE
1 onion, chopped
2 garlic cloves, minced
2 tablespoons olive oil
small pinch of chilli (hot pepper) flakes or good splash of Tabasco sauce
400 g (14 oz) tin of chopped tomatoes
1 tablespoon soft brown sugar or good squirt of tomato ketchup
½ bunch of basil, torn

1. Cook the onion and garlic in a frying pan with around a tablespoon of olive oil over a medium heat for 5–10 minutes, or until softened.

2. Transfer the cooked onion and garlic to a food processor, add the black beans, oats, harissa, oregano, vinegar, breadcrumbs and seasoning and blend until everything comes together. Pulse and don't overblend. Roll the mixture into 16–20 meatballs.

3. Heat around 1 tablespoon of olive oil in the same large frying pan over a medium to high heat, add the meatballs and cook for 10–15 minutes, turning every few minutes so all sides are browned.

4. Meanwhile, start the tomato sauce by frying the onion and garlic in the olive oil in a large saucepan over a medium heat for 5–10 minutes, or until softened. Add the remaining ingredients, fill the empty tomato tin halfway with water and add to the pan. Bring to the boil, then reduce the heat, simmer for 5–10 minutes and season.

5. When the meatballs are ready, add them to the tomato sauce and cook for 5 or so minutes (don't overstir to avoid breaking the meatballs).

6. You can serve the meatballs with spaghetti or make a meatball sub. Simply add to a large baguette, then scoop over the tomato sauce and a layer of vegan cheese. Toast open under a preheated grill (broiler) until the cheese has melted, then close the sandwich up and enjoy.

TIP
— You can shape these meatballs into burgers instead!

Homemade Pizza

MAKES 2 LARGE OR 4 SMALL PIZZAS
—

PREP TIME 1 HOUR+
COOK TIME 10 MINS

At home we would often make pizzas together as a family. Making the dough from scratch can seem a daunting task (it did for me at least), but it's surprisingly simple. You won't ever eat better pizza than a homemade one, and you can share the pizza joy with friends and family. You can use a stand mixer with a dough hook attachment, but I've also included tips if you're making it by hand.

500 g (1 lb 2 oz/4 cups) strong white bread flour, plus extra for dusting
7 g (¼ oz) sea salt
7 g (¼ oz) packet of fast-action dried yeast
12 ml (2½ teaspoons) olive oil
325 ml (11 fl oz/1⅓ cups) tepid water
polenta (cornmeal), for sprinkling under the base

FOR THE TOMATO SAUCE BASE
400–500g (14 oz–1 lb 5 oz) passata (sieved tomatoes) or 400 g (14 oz) tin of chopped tomatoes, half the juice drained off
1 tablespoon tomato purée (paste)
1 teaspoon dried Italian herbs or dried oregano
handful of basil, torn (optional)
sea salt and freshly ground black pepper

FOR THE TOPPINGS
200 g (7 oz) vegan cheese, grated, or Easy Vegan Pesto (page 108)
200 g (7 oz) shiitake mushrooms or tempeh
400–500g (14 oz–1 lb 5oz) tinned jackfruit, rinsed, drained and dried

1. Add the flour to a stand mixer fitted with a dough hook attachment together with the salt, yeast and olive oil. (Take care that the yeast and salt do not mix or touch each other, as salt can kill the active properties of yeast.)
2. Pour in the measured water and start kneading on a slow speed at first and slowly increase to a middle speed (halfway). Knead for 5 minutes, or until you have a nice elastic dough.
3. If you don't have a stand mixer, you can make the dough with your hands. Make a circle of the flour mixed with the yeast on a clean work surface. Add the oil and salt to the water and slowly pour into the centre of the circle at the same time as mixing in the flour with your hands to form a dough. Once that is done, dust the work surface with flour and knead the dough for about 10 minutes, or until it is elastic.
4. Form the dough into a ball, place in a bowl, cover with a dish towel and leave to rise for 1 hour, or until doubled in size. Place the dough in the refrigerator and leave overnight – this improves the elasticity of the dough, making it easier to stretch out.
5. Preheat a fan oven to 220°C (475°F).
6. Mix all the ingredients for the tomato sauce together in a large bowl and set aside.
7. Cut the risen dough in half (and half again if making four pizzas). On a very lightly floured work surface, roll out each piece of dough and stretch until you have the desired shape and thickness. Keep playing with the dough to stretch it out, as it will continue to expand as you play with it.
8. Place each pizza on a large baking sheet (add a sprinkle of polenta to the baking sheet first to stop the pizzas sticking), top with the tomato sauce and your desired toppings, and bake in the oven for about 10 minutes until the base is golden brown and crispy.

Butter No-chicken Curry

Alex's favourite is Indian food, and it's up there as one of mine too. Butter chicken, or traditionally *murgh makhani*, is rich, tomato-y and creamy, and easily adaptable. Simply swap the chicken for tofu, your favourite vegan chicken alternative or seitan and substitute the butter for the many vegan butters available now. The most important step is to marinate the tofu to give it depth of flavour. This is ideal for those with a milder palate or it can be made spicier with additional chilli.

SERVES 4

—

PREP TIME 1 HOUR 10 MINS
COOK TIME 20-25 MINS

FOR THE 'NO-CHICKEN' MARINADE
½ teaspoon each of ground turmeric, fenugreek leaves, ground coriander and garam masala
pinch each of chilli powder and paprika
thumb-sized piece (about 5 cm/2 in) of fresh ginger root
2 garlic cloves, minced
drizzle of vegetable oil
juice of ½ lemon
100 g (3½ oz) vegan coconut yoghurt
salt and freshly ground black pepper
600–800 g (14 oz–1 lb 5 oz) tofu (or 2 blocks), chopped into cubes, vegan chicken alternative or seitan (page 110)

FOR THE CURRY SAUCE
80 g (2¾ oz/½ cup) cashews
400 g (14 oz) tin of chopped tomatoes
2 tablespoons vegan butter or vegetable oil
1 cinnamon stick
2 cloves
2 cardamom pods
1 green chilli, finely chopped
250 ml (8 fl oz/1 cup) water
½ teaspoon each garam masala and fenugreek leaves
100 ml (3½ fl oz) coconut cream

OPTIONAL
coriander (cilantro), to serve
rice or vegan naan, to serve

1. To make the marinade, mix all the spices, ginger, garlic, oil, lemon juice and yoghurt together in a large bowl. Season with salt and pepper. Add the tofu, vegan chicken or seitan and leave to marinade for at least 1 hour, or overnight.

2. For the curry sauce, blend the cashews and tomatoes together in a blender or food processor until smooth. Set aside.

3. Heat the vegan butter or vegetable oil, cinnamon stick, cloves and cardamom in a large saucepan over a medium heat for a few minutes. Add the marinated tofu, vegan chicken or seitan, along with the marinade, and fry for 10 minutes, or until golden.

4. Add the green chilli and fry for a few more minutes.

5. Pour over the puréed tomato and cashew paste, then add the measured water and adjust if the curry needs more water. Bring to the boil, reduce the heat and simmer for 5–10 minutes.

6. Add the garam masala and fenugreek, then pour in the coconut cream and stir through.

7. Serve with coriander and rice or vegan naan.

Tofu Satay Curry

SERVES 3-4

—

PREP TIME 20 MINS
COOK TIME 30 MINS

You just cannot beat this recipe for a creamy peanut satay curry that is completely vegan. Sweet, salty, creamy and unbelievably more-ish, it has very few ingredients, making it budget-friendly, and uses foods I always have in the cupboard or refrigerator. Feel free to add some easy-to-cook vegetables, such as broccoli, spinach or sugar snap (snow) peas. I use a blender to make an extra smooth sauce, but it isn't a necessity.

400 g (14 oz) block of firm tofu
olive oil, for drizzling
1 onion, finely chopped
3 garlic cloves, finely chopped
thumb-sized piece (about
  5 cm/2 in) of fresh ginger root,
  diced
1 red chilli, finely chopped
1 tablespoon curry powder
250 ml (8 fl oz/1 cup) water
3–4 tablespoons peanut butter
400 ml (14 fl oz) tin coconut milk
1 tablespoon dark soy sauce
juice of ½ lime

FOR THE SATAY SEASONING
½ teaspoon ground coriander
½ teaspoon ground cumin
½ teaspoon ground turmeric
½ teaspoon chilli powder
1 teaspoon curry powder
1 tablespoon dark soy sauce (use
  tamari for gluten-free option)
salt and freshly ground black
  pepper

TO SERVE
150g–225g (5½–8oz/¾–1¼
  cups) basmati rice, cooked
lime wedges
handful of coriander (cilantro)
handful of peanuts
1 fresh chilli, chopped

1. Press the tofu for 5–10 minutes (see tip on page 66), then chop into bite-sized chunks.

2. Mix all the ingredients for the satay seasoning together in a large bowl. Add the tofu and mix, coating each piece of tofu.

3. Add a drizzle of oil to a large frying pan over a medium to high heat. Add the tofu with the satay seasoning and fry for 10 minutes, or until golden brown. Remove the tofu from the pan and set aside in a bowl.

4. Heat a little oil in a large saucepan over a medium heat, then add the onion, garlic, ginger, chilli and curry powder and fry, stirring constantly for 5 minutes, or until the onion is softened. Add a dash of water, if necessary.

5. Transfer the mixture to a blender and blitz with the measured water and the peanut butter. (If you don't have a blender, this step can be skipped; just add the water and peanut butter to the pan and follow the remaining steps.)

6. Return the mixture to the pan, add the coconut milk, soy sauce, lime juice and the tofu you prepared earlier and bring to the boil. Reduce the heat to a simmer and cook for 15 minutes, or until the sauce has thickened.

7. Serve the creamy satay with rice, a squeeze of lime, sprinkle of coriander, peanuts and some chopped raw chillies.

Sundried Tomato and Tahini Rigatoni

When I first made this, Alex and I devoured the entire lot in one go. Yes, that's right, pasta that serves probably six people between the two of us. It was that delicious! I love tahini as a creamy ingredient for vegan dishes and the sundried tomatoes add a rich sweetness that perfectly complements the chilli, lemon and garlic.
Feel free to swap the rigatoni for your favourite pasta shape.

SERVES 6
—
PREP TIME 10 MINS
COOK TIME 15 MINS

500 g (1 lb 2 oz) rigatoni (or gluten-free pasta)
1 tablespoon olive oil
100 g (3½ oz/⅔ cup) sundried tomatoes
3 tablespoons oil from a jar of sundried tomatoes
4 tablespoons hulled tahini (try and find the runny kind from the world foods aisle of the supermarket)
3 garlic cloves
1 teaspoon ground cumin
1 teaspoon dried oregano
juice of 1 lemon
½ teaspoon chilli (hot pepper) flakes
salt and freshly ground black pepper

1. Bring a large saucepan of salted water to the boil. Add the pasta and cook for 8–10 minutes until al dente, or according to the packet instructions. When cooked, drain, add back to the pan and drizzle with olive oil.

2. Meanwhile, add half the sundried tomatoes, the oil, tahini, garlic cloves, cumin, oregano, lemon juice, chilli flakes and salt and pepper to a food processor or blender, and blitz until smooth. Taste and adjust the seasoning, if needed. You may need to add more tahini depending on the kind you buy to make it runnier. Add a little water, if needed.

3. Roughly chop the remaining sundried tomatoes. Return the pan with the pasta to a low to medium heat, stirring through the chopped sundried tomatoes with the blended sauce and warming for a minute or two.

TIP
— The kind of tahini you use is important here, as the darker, thicker unhulled kind, while full of extra nutritious goodness and great for many reasons, is much more bitter and less runny. Using the thinner, paler hulled tahini for creamy sauces is better when substituting creams and cheeses in recipes like this.

Kao Soi

We are travelling back to Thailand for this recipe as it left a lasting impression on me and my cooking. We stayed in Chiang Mai for our entire visit, and Kao Soi could be found on every menu at all of our favourite vegan and vegetarian restaurants in the city. It was Alex's favourite, so I endeavoured to make it when we returned to the UK. A spicy, creamy soup poured over noodles and with crispy noodles on top, it is seriously yummy. You can substitute the homemade paste with a red Thai curry paste if you don't have the time, but want a similar effect. I would highly recommend making the paste, however, as you can't beat a fresh curry paste, and then you have enough for a few meals!

SERVES 4
—
PREP TIME 20 MINS
COOK TIME 55 MINS

approx. 300–400 g (10½–14 oz) block of tofu
oil, for drizzling
400 g (14 oz) noodles (udon, soba, wholewheat or your favourite to substitute for the usual egg noodles)
salt and freshly ground black pepper

FOR THE KAO SOI PASTE
2–3 fresh bird's eye chillies (these are very spicy, so base on your preference – you can seed them to reduce the heat even more)
2 shallots, roughly chopped
6 garlic cloves
1 lemongrass stalk (white part only), roughly chopped
4 lime leaves
thumb-sized piece (about 5 cm/ 2 in) of galangal or use 1 teaspoon galangal paste
thumb-sized piece (about 5 cm/ 2 in) of fresh ginger root
2 teaspoons ground turmeric (fresh would be even better)
2 teaspoons coriander (cilantro)
grated zest of 1 lime
pinch of salt
handful of coriander (cilantro) stalks

1. Press the tofu for 5–10 minutes (see tip on page 66), then chop into bite-sized chunks.
2. Add the tofu to a large frying pan or wok with a drizzle of oil. Season with salt and pepper, toss and fry over a medium heat for 15 minutes until golden brown on all sides. Remove from the pan and set aside in a bowl.
3. Meanwhile, add all the chilli paste ingredients to a food processor (or grind in a pestle and mortar) and blend together until they form a paste.
4. For the soup, add a drizzle of oil to the same pan or wok, then add a third to half of the chilli paste and cook over a medium heat for a few minutes until fragrant and it starts to colour, adding a little extra oil or splash of water if it gets too dry.
5. Pour in the vegetable stock and bring to the boil, then add the coconut milk, reserved tofu, soy sauce or tamari, and sugar. Reduce to a simmer and cook for 20–25 minutes.
6. Meanwhile, cook your choice of noodles in a large saucepan of boiling salted water for 8–10 minutes, or according to the packet instructions. Drain the noodles and rinse with cold water.
7. Divide the cooked noodles between four bowls, top with the soup and garnish with the shallots or red onion, lime wedges, coriander and crispy noodles.

TIP
— Store the remaining paste in an airtight container in the refrigerator for up to a week.

FOR THE SOUP
750 ml (25 fl oz/3 cups)
  vegetable stock
400 ml (14 fl oz) tin
  of coconut milk
3 tablespoons soy sauce (or
  tamari for a gluten-free option)
1 tablespoon soft brown or
  coconut sugar

TO GARNISH
1–2 shallots or ¼–½ red onion,
  thinly sliced
lime wedges
handful of coriander (cilantro)
  leaves, chopped
crispy noodles

Garlic Pesto Artichoke Gnocchi

SERVES 4
—
PREP TIME 35-40 MINS
COOK TIME 40 MINS

Like my Parmigiana Melanzane (page 95), we had the pleasure of enjoying a garlic pesto artichoke gnocchi on our wedding day, and it did not disappoint. Making gnocchi from scratch is surprisingly straightforward. You can, of course, buy ready-made gnocchi, but just make sure that it's egg-free.

1 kg (2 lb 4 oz) Russet or red potatoes, peeled and roughly chopped
250 g (9 oz/2 cups) plain (all-purpose) flour (you may need more depending on the potatoes, so this is an estimate), plus extra for dusting
1 teaspoon salt
olive oil, for frying
200–300g (7–10½ oz) jar artichokes, roughly chopped

FOR THE EASY VEGAN PESTO
1 bunch of basil
large glug of olive oil
5 tablespoons pine nuts
1 garlic clove
large pinch of salt
10 g (½ oz/¼ cup) nutritional yeast

1. Cook the potatoes in a large saucepan of boiling salted water for 20 minutes, or until soft.
2. Drain and mash the potatoes (or use a potato ricer) and set aside to cool.
3. Meanwhile, to make the pesto, add all the ingredients to a food processor and blitz. Alternatively, use a pestle and mortar and mash until smooth. Set aside.
4. Add the potatoes, flour and salt to a large bowl and knead together to form a dough that is no longer sticky. If the dough remains sticky, keep adding flour until it no longer sticks to your hands or the bowl.
5. Roll the dough out on a lightly floured work surface into a flattened ball shape. Cut into quarters with a sharp knife or dough scraper. Roll each quarter into a rope, about 1.5–2-cm (⅝–¾-in) thick, then cut each rope into 1.5–2 cm (⅝–¾ in) thick gnocchi dumplings.
6. These dumplings can be left as they are, or rolled along the back of a fork with your thumb to create the gnocchi ridges (you can also do this with a gnocchi board if you have one or love gnocchi enough to buy one for this recipe).
7. Bring a large saucepan of water to the boil and add the gnocchi, one by one. Cook in batches (probably around two) for 2–4 minutes until the gnocchi float to the top. Remove them with a slotted spoon, draining off any excess water, and set aside on a baking tray (pan) or cutting board.
8. When the gnocchi is cooked, drain the water from the pan, setting aside a mugful of the cooking water.
9. Heat a little olive oil in a large frying pan over a medium to high heat, add the gnocchi and pan-fry for a few minutes on each side until golden. Again, this may need doing in batches. When browned, stir through the pesto, a little of the reserved pasta water and artichokes, and serve immediately.

TIP
— For a creamy pesto dish, add 180 ml (6 fl oz/¾ cup) vegan cream
  along with the pesto.

Sticky Seitan Ribs

Seitan is a vegan meat alternative made from vital wheat gluten, which is simply the gluten removed from wheat. It can be used to recreate the texture of meat and is surprisingly simple to make. I love picking up meat alternatives from the shops, but it can be super fun to try making your own versions. Especially when you can change the spices and make it a bit different each time. You can follow the principle of this basic recipe, leave out the barbecue sauce, and just swap the spices for different versions, if you like.

SERVES 2
—
PREP TIME 15 MINS
COOK TIME 40 MINS

FOR THE BARBECUE SEITAN
120 g (4 oz) vital wheat gluten
2 tablespoons nutritional yeast
2 teaspoons smoked paprika
1 teaspoon cayenne pepper
2 teaspoons onion powder
1 teaspoon garlic powder
1 tablespoon soft brown sugar
pinch of sea salt
1 teaspoon mustard powder
180 ml (6 fl oz/¾ cup) water
1 tablespoon soy sauce
   (or tamari)
1 teaspoon liquid smoke
olive oil, for cooking
freshly ground black pepper

FOR THE BARBECUE SAUCE
   (OR USE SHOP-BOUGHT)
100 g (3½ oz) tomato ketchup
100 g (3½ oz) soft brown sugar
1 tablespoon soy sauce
2 tablespoons vegan
   Worcestershire sauce or apple
   cider vinegar
2 tablespoons hot sauce
1 teaspoon Dijon mustard
salt and freshly ground black
   pepper

1. Preheat a fan oven to 200°C (425°F). Grease and line a 20 × 20 cm (8 × 8 in) baking dish.
2. Mix all the dry ingredients for the seitan together in a large bowl. Add the measured water, soy sauce or tamari, and liquid smoke and stir through until you have a dough. Knead the dough until it comes together, for 30–60 seconds. Try not to overwork the dough, as you want it to remain pliable.
3. Flatten the dough out on a work surface, cut it in half and shape into two equal oval pieces. Add to the prepared baking dish and bake in the oven for 25–30 minutes.
4. Meanwhile, mix all the ingredients for the barbecue sauce together in a small bowl. Pour into a small saucepan and heat over a low to medium heat for a couple of minutes until bubbling.
5. Remove the seitan from the oven and generously coat each piece with the barbecue sauce.
6. Heat a large griddle pan with a little oil over a high heat. Add both pieces of seitan and fry on both sides for 2–3 minutes, or until browned. Remove from the pan and cut into slices. Drizzle over any remaining barbecue sauce, then leave the seitan to rest for 5 minutes before enjoying.

MAKE IT VEGAN

Roast Aubergine with Harissa Yoghurt

SERVES 4
—
PREP TIME 10 MINS
COOK TIME 55 MINS

Roasting aubergines (eggplants) brings out their delicious, creamy and earthy depth of flavour. Paired with the sweet spice of the harissa yoghurt this enhances the Middle Eastern and North African flavours of this dish. I love this as a main, or as a part of a larger spread or side.

4 aubergines (eggplants)
2 tablespoons olive oil
6 tablespoons plain vegan yoghurt
grated zest of ½ lemon
squeeze of lemon juice
1 small garlic clove, grated
sea salt and freshly ground black pepper
2 tablespoons pine nuts (swap for toasted sesame, pumpkin or sunflower seeds for a nut-free option)
75 g (2½ oz) vegan butter
1 tablespoon rose harissa paste
1 tablespoon chopped mint
1 red chilli, finely sliced

1. Preheat a fan oven to 190°C (400°F).
2. Pierce the aubergines three or four times, then brush with the olive oil and arrange on a large baking sheet. Roast in the oven for 45 minutes, or until the aubergines are completely soft.
3. Mix the yoghurt, lemon zest, lemon juice, garlic and a pinch of sea salt in a medium bowl. Toast the pine nuts in a small, dry frying pan over a high heat, stirring for a couple of minutes.
4. Melt the butter in the microwave in a microwaveable bowl in 10-second bursts, then stir through the harissa. Set aside.
5. Cut the aubergines in half, opening them up like a baked potato. Arrange them on a warm platter and season the inside of each one with salt and pepper.
6. Spoon the yoghurt mixture into each of the aubergine halves, then drizzle over the harissa butter. Finally, scatter over the mint, toasted pine nuts and sliced chilli, and enjoy.

Firecracker Tofu Nuggets

SERVES 2

—

PREP TIME 15-20 MINS
COOK TIME 10 MINS

An extremely delicious way to eat tofu is coating it in crispy breadcrumbs and adding some spice. Crispy on the outside and soft on the inside, these nuggets are surprisingly easy to whip up and are a great crowd-pleaser. You can even make the nuggets gluten-free by swapping out the breadcrumbs and flour for gluten-free versions.

2 firm blocks of tofu
125 g (4½ oz/1 cup) plain
   (all purpose) flour (or
   gluten-free flour)
125 ml (4¼ fl oz/½ cup)
   non-dairy milk
1 teaspoon cayenne pepper
1 teaspoon paprika
1 teaspoon ground cumin
1 teaspoon garlic granules
salt and freshly ground
   black pepper
75 g (2½ oz/¾ cup) breadcrumbs
   (either homemade or use
   shop-bought, or gluten-free
   breadcrumbs)
pinch of chilli (hot pepper) flakes
3 teaspoons sesame seeds
10 tablespoons plain
   (all-purpose) flour (or
   gluten-free flour)
vegetable oil, for frying
side salad, to serve
chips (fries) or potato wedges,
   to serve

FOR THE HARISSA YOGHURT
4 tablespoons plain vegan
   yoghurt
2 teaspoons rose harissa
grated zest of ½ lemon

1. Squeeze as much liquid from the tofu as you can or use a tofu press if you have one (see tip on page 66). Cut into roughly 2 cm (¾ in) chunks.
2. Place 5 tablespoons of the flour in a large bowl, add the milk and spices, then season with salt and pepper and mix well. Add the breadcrumbs, chilli flakes and sesame seeds to another bowl, and the remaining flour to a third.
3. Dip the tofu chunks, first in the flour, coating them on all sides, then in the flour and milk mixture, and finally in the breadcrumbs, making sure that all sides are coated.
4. Mix all the ingredients for the harissa yoghurt together in a small bowl and set aside.
5. Heat a generous amount of oil for cooking in a large frying pan (the oil should be about 2 cm/¾ in deep), then fry the tofu in batches over a medium to high heat for 5–10 minutes, or until the chunks are deep golden brown and crispy.
6. Serve with a side salad, the harissa yoghurt and chips or wedges.

TIP
— For an extra ultra-crispy coating, double dip the tofu in the flour, milk and breadcrumbs.

MAKE IT VEGAN

Coconut Beetroot Risotto

SERVES 4

—

PREP TIME 10 MINS
COOK TIME 1 HOUR

Colourful, earthy and simple, this dish is easy to put together for a super-nutritious and delicious meal for late summer and autumn (fall) when beetroot (beets) is abundant. Beetroot is probably a vegetable that I don't give enough love to, but roasting it and adding it to this risotto with the sweetness of the coconut is probably one of my favourite ways to enjoy it.

500 g (1 lb 2 oz) raw beetroot (beets), peeled and chopped into quarters
2 tablespoons olive oil
1 large onion, chopped
2 garlic cloves, finely chopped
400 ml (14 fl oz) tin of coconut milk
750 ml (25 fl oz/3 cups) hot vegetable stock
400 g (14 oz/scant 2 cups) arborio rice
100 ml (3½ fl oz/scant ½ cup) white wine
grated zest and juice of 1 orange
small bunch of parsley or coriander (cilantro), finely chopped
salt and freshly ground black pepper
1 tablespoon balsamic glaze
100 g (3½ oz) vegan Feta (see No-feta Greek Inspired Salad, page 150), to serve (optional)

1. Preheat a fan oven to 200°C (425°F).
2. Arrange the beetroot in a large baking tray (pan) and bake in the oven for 30–35 minutes until tender. Remove from the oven and transfer half the beetroot to a food processor and blitz. Set aside. Leave the rest to cool, then cut into dice.
3. Heat a large saucepan with the olive oil over a medium heat, then add the onion and garlic and cook for 10 minutes, or until softened. Mix the coconut milk with the hot stock in a jug.
4. Add the rice to the saucepan, then pour in the wine and cook for a couple of minutes until the liquid has reduced. Lower the heat and add a ladleful of the stock and coconut milk mixture. Stir constantly until the stock and coconut milk mixture has been absorbed, then add another ladleful. Keep repeating this step, and stirring, until all the stock and coconut milk mixture has been added. Add the blitzed beetroot, stir in the orange juice, zest and some of the chopped herbs, then season to taste with salt and black pepper. Keep stirring until the beetroot has heated through.
5. Arrange the cubed beetroot on top, drizzle over the balsamic glaze, sprinkle with the remaining herbs and vegan feta (if using) to serve.

TIP
— If beetroot (beet) isn't your cup of tea, swap for roasted butternut squash, (bell) peppers or courgette (zucchini).

Cauliflower and Mushroom Burgers

If you're a lover of a beef burger, it's time to try a vegan alternative. I love whipping up veggie burgers like these cauliflower and mushroom ones, which are packed with nutrients to make eating plants fun and enjoyable. The mushrooms are full of vitamin D, selenium and potassium, while the cauliflowers are bursting with vitamins C and K and folate. Plus, they're high in fibre, which we all know is great for the gut.

MAKES 4
—
PREP TIME 45 MINS
COOK TIME 25 MINS

40 g (1½ oz/⅓ cup) chickpea (gram) flour, plus extra for coating
2 tablespoons non-dairy milk
2 garlic cloves
2 portobello mushrooms
½ small to medium cauliflower (about 200 g/7 oz)
1 small onion
2 tablespoons olive oil, plus extra for frying
1 teaspoon smoked paprika
1 tablespoon parsley, chopped or 1 teaspoon dried oregano if you don't have any fresh herbs
2 tablespoons tomato purée (paste)
salt and freshly ground black pepper

TO SERVE
fresh burger buns
large green salad
tomato ketchup
Pesto Potato Salad (page 149), optional

1. In a large bowl, whisk the chickpea flour with enough milk to make a batter (a few lumps are OK), then leave to stand for 15–20 minutes.
2. Finely chop the garlic, mushrooms, cauliflower and onion (you can also blitz them in a food processor for ease).
3. Heat some olive oil in a large frying pan over a medium heat, add the garlic, mushrooms, cauliflower and onion and cook, stirring occasionally, for 10–15 minutes until the vegetables are softened and golden brown. Remove the pan from the heat and leave the mixture to cool for 5 minutes.
4. Empty the cooled vegetable mixture into the chickpea batter and add the remaining ingredients. Season to taste. Spread some flour lightly over a plate. Take about 2 tablespoons of the mixture in your hands and shape it into a ball, then flatten and arrange on the floured plate. Repeat until all the mixture has been used. This should make around four burgers.
5. Heat around a tablespoon of oil in a large frying pan, then add the burgers and cook over a medium to high heat, turning after 3–4 minutes and repeating on the other side until they are crisp on the outside. Serve inside a fresh burger bun with some salad and ketchup, on top of a big green salad, or with a side of my Pesto Potato Salad.

MAKE IT VEGAN

Vegan Paella

I have so many happy memories of enjoying paella by the beach in Mallorca, and it doesn't need seafood to transport me to the sunny shores of Spain. The colours and spices of a paella are what make it so inviting for the senses. For a twist, we are using jackfruit here to replace any seafood or meat. Jackfruit can be used in vegan dishes for that meaty, tear-apart texture.

SERVES 4
—
PREP TIME 5 MINS
COOK TIME 40 MINS

1 onion, chopped
1 red (bell) pepper, chopped
1 orange (bell) pepper, chopped
oil, for frying
3 garlic cloves, thinly sliced
1 red chilli, thinly sliced
2 teaspoons sweet smoked
  paprika
200–300 g (7–10½ oz/a punnet)
  baby button mushrooms,
  halved
4 tomatoes, chopped
400 g (14 oz) tin of jackfruit,
  drained and roughly chopped
  into quarters
300 g (10½ oz/1⅓ cups) paella
  rice
1 litre (34 fl oz/4¼ cups)
  vegetable stock
good pinch of saffron threads
salt and freshly ground black
  pepper
200 g (7 oz/1¼ cups) frozen peas
juice of 1 lemon
handful of parsley, chopped
lemon wedges, to serve

1. In a large frying pan, fry the onion and peppers in some oil over a medium heat for 5–10 minutes, or until softened.
2. Add the garlic and chilli to the pan and cook for 1–2 minutes. Add the smoked paprika and fry for another 1–2 minutes, mixing everything together.
3. Add the mushrooms, tomatoes and jackfruit to the pan along with the rice, stock and saffron. Season to taste with salt and pepper. Stir everything together to make sure it's all thoroughly mixed and bring to the boil. Once boiling, reduce the heat to a simmer and cook for 15–20 minutes until the liquid is absorbed and the rice is tender. Gently add the peas to the top, bedding them in a little to cook in the residual heat. Squeeze over the lemon and sprinkle with the parsley to finish. Serve with extra lemon wedges.

TIPS
— You can leave out the jackfruit and add a vegan meat alternative (fried first) for something extra meaty, if you like.
— Try not to overstir the paella, as the crust on the base is the best bit!

Beetroot Mushroom Wellington

A traditional wellington is the ideal vegan accompaniment to your Sunday roast. Using beetroot (beets) to create that incredible colour when you cut into the wellington, and coating it in a meaty-mushroom duxelle, makes this a show-stopping main to serve to your guests. I've made it easy so it's doable at home, without having to overthink anything, and allow the sweet beetroot and earthy mushrooms to speak for themselves.

SERVES 4
—
PREP TIME 25-30 MINS
COOK TIME 1 HOUR

2 outer leaves of 1 Savoy cabbage, stems carefully removed
320 g (11 oz) sheet of ready-rolled vegan puff pastry (Jus-Rol is vegan)
4 beetroot (beets) in brine
non-dairy milk, for brushing

FOR THE MUSHROOM DUXELLE
1 tablespoon olive oil
500 g (1 lb 2 oz) chestnut mushrooms, chopped
3 garlic cloves, finely chopped
2 tablespoons Dijon mustard
splash of soy sauce
grated zest of 1 lemon
3 tablespoons chopped thyme
salt and freshly ground black pepper

TO SERVE
vegetable gravy
mashed potatoes
green vegetables

1. Preheat a fan oven to 180°C (400°F). Line a large baking tray (pan) with baking parchment or a silicone sheet.
2. Bring a large saucepan of water to the boil, then add the cabbage leaves and blanch for a couple of minutes. Remove and add to a large bowl of cold water.
3. Meanwhile, for the duxelle, heat the olive oil in a large frying pan, add the mushrooms and fry over a medium heat for 10–15 minutes until softened.
4. Add the garlic and fry for another minute. Add the mustard, soy sauce, lemon zest and chopped thyme, and season with salt and pepper. Transfer the mixture to a food processor and blitz until very finely chopped, then set aside.
5. Drain the cabbage leaves and pat dry with a paper towel or clean dish towel.
6. Unroll the puff pastry onto the lined baking tray. Neatly place the cabbage leaves along the middle of the pastry and top with a layer of the mushroom duxelle. Next place the beetroot on top. Finally, spoon the remaining mushroom duxelle over the beetroot, packing everything in with your hands and making an even layer of duxelles around the beetroot. Make sure you leave at least a 5 cm (2 in) border around the edge of the pastry.
7. Lift and pull the pastry over the beetroot and mushroom duxelle horizontally on one side, gently stretching the pastry if necessary, then repeat on the other side to create a log. Fold the ends of the wellington under. Lightly score the top with a knife, making a criss-cross pattern (or whatever pattern you like).
8. Brush with a little non-dairy milk and bake in the oven for 35–45 minutes until golden brown. Serve with gravy, mashed potatoes and green vegetables.

Dirty Fries

My husband and I will sample every plate of vegan dirty fries on any menu we come across that features them. They're chips (fries) with the dial turned right up. It's also something we regularly recreate at home, especially when we're craving a huge feast. The 'meat' for the fries is made from walnuts and mushrooms, creating a rich and textured alternative to make them extra filthy. Of course, you can take the principle of this recipe and cheat by using frozen chips, some vegan mince and shop-bought guacamole and salsa (we often do!).

SERVES 4
—
PREP TIME 25 MINS
COOK TIME 45 MINS

1 kg (2 lb 4 oz) potatoes (preferably Maris Piper)
generous drizzle of vegetable oil, for cooking
½–1 teaspoon chilli (hot pepper) flakes
1 teaspoon paprika
100–150 g (3½–5½ oz) vegan cheese
handful of coriander (cilantro), chopped
handful of jalapeños
salt and freshly ground black pepper

FOR THE WALNUT 'MEAT'
100 g (3½ oz/1 cup) walnut halves
250 g (9 oz) mushrooms, roughly chopped
1 tablespoon dark soy sauce (or tamari for a gluten-free option)
3 garlic cloves
½ red onion, roughly chopped
¼–½ teaspoon chilli powder
1 teaspoon paprika
1 teaspoon ground cumin
½ teaspoon dried oregano
1 tablespoon liquid smoke or use barbecue sauce (optional)
sea salt and freshly ground black pepper

1. Preheat a fan oven to 200°C (425°F).
2. Chop the potatoes into the desired chip shape (my favourite is chunky chips, but wedges also work really well), and add to a large saucepan. Cover with water, bring to the boil, reduce the heat and simmer for 5 minutes to parboil.
3. Meanwhile, add a thin layer of oil to a large baking tray (pan) and heat in the oven.
4. Drain the potatoes in a colander, shake to fluff up, then leave to steam for 5 minutes.
5. Remove the baking tray from the oven and tip in the potatoes (being careful that you don't splash the oil on yourself as it will be very hot). Sprinkle over the chilli flakes and paprika, and season with salt and pepper. Turn the potatoes with a spatula to coat evenly. Roast in the oven for 15 minutes, turn over and cook for another 15 minutes, or until golden brown and crispy.
6. While the chips cook, prepare your walnut 'meat', salsa and guacamole.
7. Add all the walnut 'meat' ingredients to a food processor, season with salt and pepper and blitz in bursts until combined to form a mince-like texture. Taste and adjust the seasoning.
8. In a large frying pan, heat a little oil and fry the walnut 'meat' over a medium heat for 5–10 minutes to crisp up. Set aside.
9. Add all the salsa ingredients to a medium bowl and mix. Season with salt and pepper, then taste and adjust the seasoning, if needed.
10. Mash the avocado in a bowl, add the coriander, lime juice and zest, and season generously with salt and pepper.
11. When the chips are ready, arrange the walnut 'meat' over the top, add with a layer of vegan cheese. Return to the oven for another 5 minutes, or until the cheese has melted.
12. Serve in a large dish for sharing, or divide among plates, and top with the salsa and guacamole, plus a sprinkling of coriander and jalapeños.

FOR THE SALSA
2–3 large tomatoes, finely chopped
¼–½ red onion, finely chopped
½ red chilli, finely chopped (can
    be left out or seeded if you
    prefer it less spicy)
juice of 1 lime
handful of coriander (cilantro),
    finely chopped

FOR THE QUICK GUACAMOLE
1 avocado, peeled and stoned
handful of coriander (cilantro),
    chopped
grated zest and juice of 1 lime
salt and freshly ground pepper

Nibbles

& Bites

Potato Skin Crisps p. 138

Sesame Cheese Twists p. 133

Spicy Nuts p. 137

Un-sausage Rolls p. 130

Spicy Pickled Avocado p. 134

Un-sausage Rolls

MAKES 6-8
—
PREP TIME 25-30 MINS
COOK TIME 45 MINS

We all love a sausage roll, and actually when I first went vegan, the Linda McCartney vegan sausage rolls were one of the few things I could find in most supermarkets that tasted truly like the real deal. We had them all the time, especially at Christmas! They're also very easy to make from scratch at home, using some ready-rolled puff pastry (my fave!), tofu and some onion chutney for sweetness.

400 g (14 oz) block of tofu
1 red onion, finely chopped
drizzle of olive oil
2 tablespoons fresh
  breadcrumbs
1 tablespoon soy sauce
1 teaspoon salt
1 teaspoon freshly ground
  black pepper
1 tablespoon nutritional yeast
1 tablespoon vegetable oil
squirt of tomato ketchup
1 vegan beef stock cube
2 tablespoons caramelised
  onion chutney
320 g (11 oz) sheet of ready-
  rolled vegan puff pastry
  (Jus-Rol is vegan), cold out of
  the refrigerator
3 tablespoons non-dairy milk
handful of sesame seeds, for
  sprinkling (optional)

1. Preheat a fan oven to 200°C (425°F). Line a baking tray (pan) with baking parchment or a silicone sheet.
2. Press the tofu in a tofu press (see tip on page 66), or between something heavy (using some paper towels between two plates and topping with some heavy cookbooks usually works well for pressing tofu).
3. Fry the onion in the olive oil in a small frying pan over a medium heat for 15 minutes, or until softened and caramelised.
4. Meanwhile, add the tofu and all the other ingredients, except the pastry, milk and sesame seeds, to a food processor. When the onions are ready, add them to the food processor and blend until the mixture comes together.
5. Open out the puff pastry on a work surface and cut across to make two rectangles.
6. Divide the sausage mixture in half, arrange in the centre of each rectangle of pastry and shape into a log with your hands, leaving a gap around the edge. Brush the edges of the pastry with the milk, then fold and join the pastry over the middle of the sausage mixture on both sides to form a large sausage roll. Flip the roll over, so that the seam is underneath. Brush the top lightly with milk.
7. Cut into 5 cm (2 in) rolls (or whatever size you like), and arrange them individually on the lined baking sheet. Sprinkle with sesame seeds (if using).
8. Bake in the oven for 25–30 minutes until golden, then leave to cool for 10 minutes and enjoy. Store in the fridge for up to three days, or in the freezer for two months.

TIP
— You can use shop-bought vegan sausages for the filling instead of the tofu. Just remove the skins.

Sesame Cheese Twists

Twists of cheesy sesame goodness, these are ideal to serve at a party, enjoy for a celebration or just as a delicious homemade snack when you're craving something uber cheesy. They only use a handful of ingredients and can be adapted with different flavours and spices to vary them each time.

MAKES 6
–
PREP TIME 10-15 MINS
COOK TIME 12 MINS

320 g (11 oz) sheet of ready-rolled vegan puff pastry (Jus-Rol is vegan)
plain (all-purpose) flour, for dusting
50 g (1¾ oz) vegan butter, melted (plus extra butter for greasing)
100 g (3½ oz) vegan cheese, grated
25 g (1 oz/3 tablespoons) sesame seeds
½ teaspoon garlic powder
sea salt
chilli (hot pepper) flakes, for sprinkling

1. Preheat a fan oven to 200°C (425°F). Lightly grease a large baking sheet or line with a silicone sheet.
2. Unfold the puff pastry sheet onto a lightly floured work surface.
3. Combine the melted butter, grated vegan cheese, sesame seeds and garlic powder in a large bowl.
4. Cut the pastry in half vertically and spread the cheese mixture on one half of the pastry, top with the other half of pastry, then roll out with a rolling pin until about 5 mm (¼ in) thick. Cut the pastry into approximately 12 strips.
5. Gently wrap two pastry strips together to create a twist and arrange on the prepared baking sheet or silicone sheet (if using). Try and create a tighter twist to ensure the twists don't explode or lose their shape in the oven.
6. Bake for 12 minutes, or until melted and golden brown. Sprinkle with sea salt and chilli flakes and serve hot or cold.

Spicy Pickled Avocado

MAKES 1 JAR

—

PREP TIME 4 HOURS
COOK TIME 10 MINS

I absolutely love pickles. Recently, I started trying to make my own at home after being gifted a book by my friend all about pickling foods. The vinegar gives any fruit or vegetable a delicious tang that you can enjoy straight out of the jar, or alongside your favourite salads and sandwiches. It's super simple to do and a fun way to experiment with food.

225 ml (7½ fl oz/scant 1 cup) distilled white vinegar
225 ml (7½ fl oz/scant 1 cup) water
75 g (2½ oz/⅓ cup) sugar
1 tablespoon sea salt
1 teaspoon chilli (hot pepper) flakes
grated zest of 1 lemon
6 black peppercorns
1 teaspoon coriander seeds
6 sprigs of coriander (cilantro)
2 unripe avocados, peeled, stoned and thinly sliced

1. Gently heat the vinegar, water, sugar and salt in a small saucepan over a medium heat, stirring frequently for 3–5 minutes, or until the sugar has dissolved. Remove from the heat and leave to cool.
2. Add the chilli flakes, lemon zest, peppercorns, coriander seeds, sprigs of coriander and avocado slices to a sterilised jar.
3. Pour the cooled pickling mixture into the jar and seal tightly with a lid. Store in the refrigerator for at least 4 hours before digging in.

TIP
— To sterilise a jar, make sure you soak it in boiling water, or run it through a dishwasher on a high heat.

MAKE IT VEGAN

Spicy Nuts

SERVES 10+

—

PREP TIME 10 MINS
COOK TIME 10-15 MINS

These spicy nuts are packed with vitamins, proteins and fats, with added sweetness and spice, making them even tastier and more inviting than anything you can buy in the shop.

500 g (1 lb 2 oz/3½ cups) mixed nuts
1½ teaspoons ground cumin
1 teaspoon cayenne pepper
½ teaspoon ground cinnamon
2 tablespoons olive oil
2 tablespoons soft light brown sugar
1–2 teaspoons sea salt

1. Line a large baking sheet with baking parchment or a silicone sheet.
2. Heat a large frying pan over a medium heat, add the nuts and toast them, making sure you move them around so they don't burn. Don't leave the pan for a minute – you need to keep watching the nuts.
3. Add the spices and toss the nuts about again, making sure they are all thoroughly coated.
4. Add the olive oil and sugar and stir again to mix. When the nuts have darkened a little and are slicked with the sugary spice mix, tip them out quickly onto the lined baking sheet. Spread the nuts out, then sprinkle over the sea salt. Leave to cool a little, then serve in bowls, or leave to cool completely and store in an airtight container for up to two weeks.

TIP
— Try garlic granules, onion powder, dried mixed herbs, and salt and pepper for something different. Or paprika, onion powder, garlic powder, chilli powder, brown sugar, and salt and pepper for a barbecue flavour.

Potato Skin Crisps

SERVES 4
—

PREP TIME 5 MINS
COOK TIME 15 MINS

Don't throw away that potato peel but turn it into crisps (potato chips)! A great way to reduce food waste and make the most of your ingredients.

---

potato peel from 4 potatoes
vegetable oil, for drizzling
salt and freshly ground black pepper
optional seasoning (cumin, paprika, chilli/hot pepper flakes)

1. Preheat a fan oven to 200°C (425°F).
2. Toss the potato peel into a large baking tray (pan) and drizzle with oil. Season with salt and pepper (and seasoning and spices, if you like), then, using your hands, evenly distribute the oil and flavourings throughout the potato peel. Spread the pieces of peel over the baking tray, making sure they are evenly spaced.
3. Bake in the oven for 8–15 minutes, turning halfway through cooking, until crispy and brown. Serve sprinkled with a little extra salt.

140–161

On the

Side

Pesto Potato Salad p. 149

Sizzling Homemade Baked Beans p. 154

Cheesy Garlic Bread Rings p. 156

No-feta Greek Inspired Salad p. 150

Curried Chips p. 153

Garlic and Herb Pesto
Braided Bread p. 144

Lemon Turmeric Rice p. 159

Celeriac Gratin (Dauphinoise) p. 160

Garlic and Herb Pesto Braided Bread

A total showstopper, this plaited (braided) bread is absolutely stunning, with basil and parsley butter swirled through a warm golden dough. It looks very impressive, but the plaited shape is only a few twists and preparation is surprisingly simple. You can use this basic recipe to try out a sweet version with chocolate spread or cinnamon and sugar instead.

SERVES 6
—
PREP TIME 3+ HOURS
COOK TIME 30 MINS

500 g (1 lb 2 oz/4 cups) white bread flour, plus extra for dusting
1 teaspoon salt
1 tablepoon golden caster (superfine) sugar
7 g (¼ oz) packet of fast-action dried yeast
60 ml (2 fl oz/¼ cup) olive oil, plus extra for oiling and 2 tablespoons for brushing
250 ml (8 fl oz/1 cup) non-dairy milk (I used oat milk)

FOR THE FILLING
75 g (2½ oz) vegan butter
3 garlic cloves, minced
3 tablespoons finely chopped basil
1 tablespoon finely chopped parsley
2 tablespoons nutritional yeast
1 teaspoon dried oregano
good pinch of sea salt

1. Add the flour to a stand mixer, together with the salt, sugar, yeast and oil, making sure that the yeast and salt do not mix or touch each other by adding to opposite sides of the bowl, as salt can kill the active properties of yeast.

2. Pour in the milk and start kneading. Keep the machine on for 5 minutes, or until you have a nice elastic dough. Roll the dough into a ball, return it to the bowl, cover with a dish towel, and leave to rise in a warm spot for 1–2 hours until doubled in size. You can also make the dough by hand following step 3 of my Homemade Pizza recipe on page 99.

3. Meanwhile, mix all the ingredients for the filling together in a large bowl and set aside.

4. Turn the dough out onto a lightly floured work surface and roll it out into a rectangle (don't make the rectangle too long). Spread the filling all over the dough, leaving a 1 cm (½ in) edge around three of the sides and a 3 cm (1¼ in) edge along one of the longer sides.

5. Roll the dough into a log shape, starting lengthways from the side with a 1 cm (½ in) gap, over to the side with the 3 cm (1¼ in) gap. Pinching the ends together, turn the log over so that the fold is underneath.

6. Using a sharp knife, slice the log in the centre lengthways to reveal the filling. Pinch the ends and roll each piece over so the filling is facing upwards. Pick up both halves and plait (braid) them tightly together. Dampen both ends, pinch and tuck under.

7. Carefully place the dough in a lightly oiled 450 g (1 lb) loaf tin (squish the plait to be shorter if needs be). Cover with a dish towel and leave to prove for 1 hour in a warm spot.

8. Preheat a fan oven to 180°C (400°F). Lightly brush the top of the plait with the olive oil and bake in the oven for 30 minutes, or until golden brown (keep an eye on it because ovens vary). Leave the bread to cool for 5 minutes and then turn out onto a wire rack to cool further before serving. Serve warm and share!

MAKE IT VEGAN

Pesto Potato Salad

SERVES 4
—
PREP TIME 15 MINS
COOK TIME 15 MINS

A classic potato salad was always served at barbecues when I was growing up. I was never a fan of shop-bought, but my mum's was seriously tasty. Using vegan mayonnaise (or olive oil) and adding a dollop of Easy Vegan Pesto (page 108) makes this a unique take on the traditional recipe.

500 g (1 lb 2 oz) new potatoes, cut into 2–3 cm (¾–1¼ in) chunks
4–5 spring onions (scallions), finely sliced
grated zest and juice of 1 lemon
2–3 tablespoons Easy Vegan Pesto (page 108) or use shop-bought
2 tablespoons vegan mayonnaise or plain vegan yoghurt
salt and freshly ground black pepper

1. Add the potatoes to a large saucepan of slightly salted water and bring to the boil. Reduce the heat and simmer for 10–15 minutes until softened.
2. While the potatoes are cooking, mix all the remaining ingredients together in a large bowl.
3. Once the potatoes are ready, drain and leave to steam in the colander for 5–10 minutes, shaking occasionally.
4. Add the potatoes to the bowl with the spring onion mixture, taste and adjust the seasoning if necessary, and serve.

● GLUTEN-FREE   ● NUT-FREE

No-feta Greek Inspired Salad

This Greek-inspired salad involves a vegan version of feta using tofu and agar agar to recreate the cheese. Agar agar can be found in some supermarkets and is a jelly-like substance and a plant-based gelatine made from algae. It works well in this case to set the cheese into a solid block. You can also omit the agar agar for a soft spreadable vegan 'cheese'. Pair the feta with the classic Greek salad ingredients for a refreshing summer salad.

SERVES 6-8

—

PREP TIME 20-25 MINS
COOK TIME 1-2 MINS

FOR THE FETA
400 g (14 oz) block of firm tofu
40–60 ml (1½–2 fl oz/¼ cup) olive oil
80 ml (3 fl oz/⅓ cup) water
60 ml (2 fl oz/¼ cup) olive brine juice
grated zest and juice of 1 lemon
2 tablespoons apple cider vinegar
2 tablespoons nutritional yeast
1 garlic clove
1 teaspoon dried oregano
2½ teaspoons sea salt
¼ teaspoon freshly ground black pepper
1 tablespoon agar agar powder
240 ml (8 fl oz/1 cup) water

FOR THE SALAD
1 cucumber
½ red onion, sliced
2 large vine tomatoes, cut into wedges
50 g (1¾ oz/⅓ cup) black Kalamata olives, pitted
small handful of mint, chopped
1 teaspoon dried oregano
drizzle of olive oil
juice of ½ lemon
salt and freshly ground black pepper

1. To make the feta, add all the ingredients, except the agar agar powder and measured water, to a food processor and blend. Taste and adjust the seasoning, if needed.
2. Prepare a 20 × 20 cm (8 × 8 in) square baking dish.
3. Add the measured water and agar agar powder to a large saucepan. Bring to the boil, stirring constantly. Once boiling, set a timer for 1 minute and continue to stir.
4. When the minute is up, and working quickly, add the agar agar mixture to the food processor and blitz. As soon as the mixture is smooth, pour it into the prepared pan or dish and smooth the top. Make sure you do all of this as quickly as possible, as the agar agar sets fast.
5. Leave the feta in the refrigerator for 15 minutes until set. Using a knife, loosen the sides, then tip it onto a cutting board and slice into cubes. Set aside.
6. To make the salad, slice the cucumber in half lengthways, remove the inside with a spoon (this is optional) and cut into slices. Add to a large bowl with the remaining salad ingredients and the plant-powered feta, then season to taste and toss together to coat everything thoroughly. Enjoy.

Curried Chips

Every time I make these chips (fries) I want to have them again the next day. They're fluffy and comforting, and the curry powder brings the chip shop home. Parboiling the potatoes first and allowing them to steam is key to making the chips extra fluffy.

SERVES 4

—

PREP TIME 15 MINS
COOK TIME 40-45 MINS

500 g (1 lb 2 oz) white potatoes (Maris Piper are best), peeled and cut into chips (fries)
vegetable oil, for cooking
about 2 tablespoons curry powder
salt and freshly ground black pepper

FOR THE CURRY KETCHUP
60 ml (2 fl oz/¼ cup) tomato ketchup
1 teaspoon curry powder

1. Preheat a fan oven to 220°C (475°F).
2. Add the chips to a large saucepan of salted water and bring to the boil. Reduce the heat and simmer for 10 minutes. Drain the chips in a colander and shake around to fluff up. Leave to steam for 5 minutes.
3. Meanwhile, add a generous amount of vegetable oil to a large baking tray (so you have approximately a 5 mm/¼ in layer of oil at the bottom of the tray). Heat the oil in the oven while the chips steam.
4. Add the chips to the hot oil and stir through (please be very careful as the oil will be very hot and may spit). Season with the curry powder (the measurement here is approximate, so if you want more, add more!) and a generous helping of salt and pepper. Turn the chips over and mix until they are evenly coated.
5. Bake in the oven for 30–35 minutes, turning once halfway through the cooking, until golden brown. Serve with curry ketchup, which is literally ketchup stirred through with curry powder.

TIP
— For added spice, sprinkle over some chilli powder.

Sizzling Homemade Baked Beans

We love our baked beans in the UK. Out of the tin is always delicious, but so is making your own. Haricot (navy) beans are the main ingredient, mixed with some sweetness from the maple syrup and tomato ketchup, smokiness from the paprika, and with some extra sizzle from the cumin and chilli (hot pepper) flakes. Enjoy with your breakfast on toast, or as a delicious lunch with a side of vegetables.

SERVES 4

—

PREP TIME 10 MINS
COOK TIME 40 MINS

400 g (14 oz) tin of haricot (navy) beans
2 garlic cloves, chopped
500 ml (17 fl oz/generous 2 cups) vegetable stock
400 g (14 oz) cherry tomatoes, halved, or use tinned
1 tablespoon maple syrup
2 tablespoons tomato purée (paste)
1 tablespoon tomato ketchup
1 tablespoon red wine vinegar
1 teaspoon smoked paprika
1 tablespoon ground cumin
½ teaspoon chilli (hot pepper) flakes (optional)
salt and freshly ground black pepper
toast or jacket potatoes, to serve

1. Add the beans, garlic, vegetable stock, tomatoes and maple syrup to a large saucepan with a dash of water and bring to the boil. Reduce the heat to a simmer and cook for up to 30 minutes, or until the mixture has thickened.

2. Add the tomato purée, ketchup, vinegar, spices, chilli flakes (if using) and season to taste with salt and pepper. Cook for another 5–10 minutes until you have the perfect baked bean texture. Serve on toast or a jacket potato.

Cheesy Garlic Bread Rings

SERVES 4-6

—

PREP TIME 2-3 HOURS
COOK TIME 25-30 MINS

This bread is ideal when you're having a gathering, as it looks great on the table and will serve a lot of people. Plus, it's super easy to do. Making any kind of dough doesn't need to be complicated, even though it can seem intimidating. These garlic bread rings are very straightforward to make; they just take some time to prove. And I can guarantee you won't regret taking the time to make them yourself.

FOR THE DOUGH
500 g (1 lb 2 oz/4 cups) white bread flour, plus extra for dusting
7 g (¼ oz) packet of fast-action dried yeast
1 teaspoon caster (superfine) sugar
1 teaspoon salt
15 ml (½ fl oz/1 tablespoon) olive oil
150 ml (5 fl oz/scant ⅔ cup) unsweetened vegan milk, at room temperature
175 ml (6 fl oz/¾ cup) lukewarm water
spray oil, for greasing
150 g (5½ oz) vegan cheese, grated

FOR THE GARLIC BUTTER
50 g (1¾ oz) vegan butter
2 garlic cloves, grated
pinch of sea salt

1. To make the dough, add the flour, then the yeast and sugar to a large bowl or a stand mixer fitted with a dough hook attachment. Add the salt to the other side of the bowl (salt and yeast mustn't mix, as the salt will kill the yeast), then add the olive oil, milk and lukewarm water. Knead for about 5 minutes. If kneading by hand, knead on a lightly floured work surface for 10 minutes, or until the dough is soft and elastic.
2. Roll the dough into a ball, return to the bowl, cover with a dish towel and leave to rise for 1–2 hours in a warm spot until doubled in size.
3. Remove the dough from the bowl and lightly press it all over to remove the air. Cut in half and roll into two balls, then cover with a dish towel and leave to rest at room temperature for 10 minutes.
4. To make the garlic butter, mix the butter, garlic and salt in a small bowl and set aside.
5. Lightly grease two 20 cm (8 in) cake tins (pans).
6. Roll out one ball to make a 35 × 20 cm (14 × 8 in) rectangle. Spread a third of the garlic butter all over the rectangle, then half the vegan cheese and roll up along the longer side. Repeat with the second ball. You will have two logs of dough. Pinch the seams to seal. With the seam underneath, carefully cut each log into 2–3 cm (¾–1¼ in) rolls almost all the way through.
7. Gently lift one of the dough logs and transfer to the prepared cake tin. Arrange the log in a ring inside the tin. Repeat with the second log, so you have a ring in each tin.
8. Spread the remaining third of garlic butter over the top of the rings, cover with a dish towel and leave to rest in a warm spot for 30 minutes.
9. Preheat a fan oven to 220°C (390°F).
10. Bake in the oven for 25 minutes, or until golden. Remove from the tins, transfer to a wire rack and leave to cool for 5–10 minutes, then enjoy by tearing each garlic ball from the rings.

MAKE IT VEGAN

Lemon Turmeric Rice

Adding lemon and turmeric to your rice is something different to do when you need an accompaniment to a main dish. The turmeric gives the rice a beautiful colour and the lemon a tangy zest. There are different kinds of lemon rice from opposite sides of the world, so I've taken some inspiration from various examples I've tried and loved.

SERVES 4

—

PREP TIME 20-25 MINS
COOK TIME 20-30 MINS

---

400 g (14 oz/scant 2 cups) long-grain rice
glug of olive oil
1 small onion, chopped
½ teaspoon mustard seeds
1 garlic clove, finely chopped
grated zest and juice of 2 lemons
600 ml (20 fl oz/2½ cups) vegetable stock
pinch of sea salt
½ teaspoon ground turmeric
handful of chopped parsley or coriander (cilantro), to serve

1. Wash the rice until the water is clear (either in a sieve/fine mesh strainer under running water, or by filling a pan/bowl with water, swirling with your fingers, draining and repeating). Soak in a generous amount of cold water in a bowl for 15–20 minutes, then drain.
2. Heat a large glug of olive oil in a large saucepan with a lid over a medium heat, then add the onion, mustard seeds and garlic, and fry for 5–10 minutes, or until the onion is translucent. Pour in the rice and toss to coat.
3. Next, add the lemon juice, vegetable stock, salt and turmeric and bring to the boil. Reduce the heat to low, cover with the lid and cook for 20 minutes, or until the rice has absorbed the liquid.
4. Remove from the heat, keep the lid on and leave to steam for another 10 minutes.
5. Fluff up the rice with a fork, stir through most of the lemon zest and parsley or coriander, then serve sprinkled with the remaining zest and herbs. Enjoy.

Celeriac Gratin (Dauphinoise)

Dauphinoise was always a luxury for me when I was younger. If it was on a menu while I was out for dinner or on holiday, I'd always order it. If my mum told me we were having it for dinner, I just couldn't wait. For this version, I wanted to add celeriac (celery root) because it is an underrated vegetable that brings a sweetness to the potatoes. I use a mandolin to slice my potatoes and celeriac as finely as possible, but if you don't have one, try your best to get the slices no more than 5 mm (¼ in) thick.

SERVES 4-6
—
PREP TIME 25 MINS
COOK TIME 1-1½ HOURS

FOR THE GRATIN
350 ml (12 fl oz/1½ cups) non-dairy milk
250 ml (8 fl oz/1 cup) vegan cream
1 tablespoon Dijon mustard
few sprigs of thyme, leaves picked and finely chopped
2 garlic cloves, grated
good grating of nutmeg
sea salt and freshly ground black pepper
1 medium celeriac (celery root), peeled
4 medium to large potatoes, peeled
1 large onion, thinly sliced

OPTIONAL
grated vegan cheese, for the topping

1. Preheat a fan oven to 180°C (400°F).
2. Mix the milk, cream, mustard, thyme, grated garlic and nutmeg together in a large bowl and season with salt and pepper.
3. Thinly slice the celeriac and potatoes with a mandolin (or use a sharp knife to cut slices less than 5 mm/¼ in thick), making sure to watch your fingers.
4. Form a layer of overlapping celeriac slices in the base of an ovenproof gratin dish, measuring about 20 × 20 cm (8 × 8 in). Spoon over a little of the milk and cream mixture, then repeat the process with a layer of potato slices and sprinkle some of the onion over. Repeat until you have used up all of the vegetables.
5. Finish by pouring over the remaining cream mixture, then add a good grinding of black pepper and sprinkle over the vegan cheese (if using).
6. Place the gratin dish on a baking tray (pan) to catch any sauce that may bubble over and bake in the oven for 1–1½ hours until the vegetables are tender (check by putting a knife through). Keep an eye on the gratin to make sure the top isn't getting too brown. If it is, place some baking parchment or kitchen foil loosely on the top.
7. Remove from the oven and leave to cool slightly for 10 minutes, then serve.

ON THE SIDE

162-185

Sweets

& Baking

Biscoff Brownies p. 166

Choc a Choc Chocolate Cake p. 180

Carrot Cake p. 176

Caramel Truffles p. 179

Chocolate Spread Cheesecake p. 170

Orange Chocolate Shortbread p. 169

Tiffin p. 174

Alex's Bread p. 182

Fluffy Lemon Sponge Cake p. 173

Biscoff Brownies

Like many of my recipes, I look back to my childhood for inspiration. I made brownies constantly as a teenager, and I became a self-proclaimed expert at baking the best brownies ever. They have to be perfectly gooey, not too spongy and with just the right amount of chocolate and sweetness. Recently, I've been adding Lotus Biscoff biscuits and biscuit spread, as these make the brownies magically accidentally vegan! Using chia seeds instead of eggs provides the binding ingredient and is a great hack for vegan baking.

MAKES 16

—

PREP TIME 15-20 MINS
COOK TIME 30-35 MINS

3 chia eggs (1:3 ratio chia to water: 3 tablespoons chia seeds, 9 tablespoons water)
115 g (4 oz) vegan butter
200 g (7 oz) vegan dark chocolate with at least 70% cocoa solids
200 g (7 oz/1 cup) soft brown sugar
1 teaspoon vanilla extract
100 g (3½ oz/generous ¾ cup) plain (all-purpose) flour
25 g (1 oz/scant ¼ cup) cocoa (unsweetened chocolate) powder
½ teaspoon salt
90 g (3¼ oz/½ cup) vegan dark chocolate chips
150 g (5½ oz) Biscoff Lotus biscuits (cookies), roughly chopped or broken
splash of soy milk (optional)
½ × 400 g (14 oz) jar of Biscoff biscuit spread

1. Preheat a fan oven to 180°C (400°F) and line a 20 × 20 cm (8 × 8 in) oven dish with baking parchment.
2. Prep the chia eggs by adding the chia seeds to a small bowl with the water, putting in the refrigerator and leaving to set until thick and gel-like.
3. Melt the butter and chocolate in a medium saucepan over a medium heat, stirring constantly and making sure the mixture doesn't burn. Remove the pan from the heat, pour into a large bowl and leave for 5 minutes or until cool.
4. Whisk the sugar and vanilla into the cooled chocolate butter mix, then whisk in a third of the chia eggs at a time. Fold in the flour, cocoa powder and salt. Finally, fold in the chocolate chips and most of the Biscoff biscuits (saving some for the topping) and a splash of milk, if needed.
5. Pour the batter into the lined oven dish and add dollops of biscoff spread throughout. Optional for decoration: use a cocktail stick (toothpick) to swirl the spread. You can now add the extra bits of biscuit on top for decoration, if you like. Bake in the oven for 30–35 minutes until the brownie comes away at the edges.
6. Leave to cool in the oven dish, then cut into slices and enjoy. The brownies can be stored in an airtight container for up to a week in the refrigerator, or three to four days at room temperature.

TIP
— You can swap the Biscoff spread for vegan Nutella, chocolate spread or peanut butter.

SWEETS & BAKING

MAKE IT VEGAN

Orange Chocolate Shortbread

The butter in shortbread is what gives it that delicious crumbly texture, but swapping dairy butter for a vegan butter can replicate the taste really well. Going to university in Scotland meant I enjoyed a lot of shortbread, and it was my dad's favourite growing up too. This recipe is actually my mum's (because of my dad's love for shortbread) and the orange and chocolate will make it impossible not to keep going back for more.

MAKES 18–20

—

PREP TIME 50 MINS
COOK TIME 15 MINS

200 g (7 oz) vegan butter
1 teaspoon vanilla extract
100 g (3½ oz/scant ½ cup) caster (superfine) sugar, plus extra for sprinkling
300 g (10½ oz/scant 2½ cups) plain (all-purpose) flour (or gluten-free flour)
grated zest of 1 orange
50 g (1¾ oz) vegan dark chocolate with at least 70% cocoa solids, chopped into small pieces, or use chocolate chips

1. Whisk the butter, vanilla extract and sugar together in a large bowl until pale, or use a stand mixer fitted with a whisk attachment. Sift and stir in the flour, then add the orange zest and, finally, the chocolate and mix into a dough. This dough will be crumbly and shouldn't be overworked. Wrap and cover in cling film (plastic wrap), then leave to chill in the refrigerator for at least 30 minutes to harden.
2. Preheat a fan oven to 160°C (350°F) and line a baking sheet with baking parchment or a silicone sheet.
3. Roll the chilled dough out on a work surface to about 5 mm (¼ in) thickness, then cut into small circles with a circular pastry cutter.
4. Transfer the shapes to the lined baking sheet and sprinkle with a little sugar. Bake for 12–15 minutes until golden brown at the edges, turning halfway through to ensure even baking.
5. Leave to cool for 10–15 minutes before serving, so that the shortbread hardens. Store in an airtight container for a week.

Chocolate Spread Cheesecake

Every Christmas my mum makes a chocolate torte or cheesecake, and so when I came home at the end of university proclaiming I was vegan, she quickly veganised a favourite recipe. It has minimal ingredients and is a real crowd-pleaser. You just need to find some vegan alternatives, including vegan chocolate spread and vegan cream cheese.

SERVES 12

–

PREP TIME 40 MINS

250 g (9 oz) Biscoff biscuits (cookies), or use gluten- or soy-free biscuits
75 g (2½ oz) vegan spread
400 g (14 oz) vegan chocolate spread (I used Nature's Store)
handful of chopped nuts (almonds or hazelnuts work well)
500 g (1 lb 2 oz) vegan cream cheese
60 g (2 oz/½ cup) icing (powdered) sugar

1. Break the biscuits into a food processor. Add the vegan spread and 1 tablespoon of the chocolate spread and blend until everything is combined into a sandy mixture.
2. Add a generous handful of nuts to the mix and continue to blend for a few minutes. Don't worry about there being a few lumps, as this will add to the crunch.
3. Pour the base mixture into a 23 cm (9 in) springform tin (pan) and press in with the back of a spoon. Once evenly pressed, leave to set in the refrigerator for 30 minutes.
4. Add the vegan cream cheese to a large bowl, sift over the icing sugar and stir together gently. Add the remaining chocolate spread and continue to beat until all the ingredients are mixed together.
5. Pour the chocolate spread mixture over the set base and smooth neatly with a tablespoon. Refrigerate for at least 4 hours, or overnight until the cheesecake has set. Serve cold from the refrigerator. This can be stored in the refrigerator for three to four days.

TIPS
— For the cream cheese, you want to find a vegan cream cheese that's thicker in texture.
— Make sure you don't overbeat the chocolate spread mixture as you want it to stay firm.
— Feel free to top the cheesecake with some chopped nuts, or decorate with fresh raspberries.

Fluffy Lemon Sponge Cake

SERVES 12

—

PREP TIME 20 MINS
COOK TIME 30 MINS

This lemon cake is refreshing, light and fluffy. Vinegar is one of the ingredients I use regularly in vegan baking. But don't worry, it doesn't taste like vinegar once cooked! The bright and zesty lemon flavour is a favourite for me in a cake, and you really wouldn't know it's vegan.

---

150 ml (5 fl oz/scant ⅔ cup) vegetable oil, plus extra for greasing
400 g (14 oz/3¼ cups) self-raising (self-rising) flour
300 g (10½ oz/1⅓ cups) golden caster (superfine) sugar
1½ teaspoons baking powder
250 ml (8 oz/1 cup) water
1 teaspoon vanilla extract
zest of 1½ lemons

FOR THE LEMON BUTTERCREAM
300 g (10½ oz/2 ½ cups) icing (powdered) sugar
200 g (7 oz) vegan butter or margarine
zest and juice of 1 lemon
1–2 tablespoons non-dairy milk

1. Preheat a fan oven to 180°C (400°F). Grease two 20 cm (8 in) cake tins (pans) and line the bases with baking parchment.
2. Sift the flour into a large bowl and add the sugar and baking powder. Add the water, vanilla and lemon zest and whisk by hand until combined, taking care not to overmix; tiny lumps are fine.
3. Divide the batter evenly between the prepared cake tins and bake in the oven for 30 minutes, or until cooked. Check by inserting a skewer into the centre of the cakes and if it comes out clean, they are done.
4. Leave to cool in the tins for 5 minutes, then carefully turn the cakes out onto a wire rack and leave to completely cool until ready to ice (frost).
5. To make the buttercream, sift half of the icing sugar into a bowl, add the butter or margarine, and beat with a whisk until light and fluffy. Whisk in the remaining icing sugar, the lemon zest and juice, and the milk.
6. Spread some of the buttercream onto one of the cake halves, then sandwich both cake halves together. Use the remaining buttercream to decorate the cake, then add an extra sprinkling of lemon zest.

TIPS
— I used vinegar and baking powder as a substitute for eggs, as well as to help the cake rise – 1 tablespoon of vinegar mixed with 1 teaspoon of baking powder per egg is a good guideline when converting cake recipes.
— The tip for a fluffy vegan sponge is not to overmix. As soon as the mixture comes together, stop! The more you mix, the more the gluten in the flour develops and that's what will make the cake dense.
— It's also important to make sure that all the ingredients are at room temperature when baking.

Tiffin

MAKES 8-10 BARS

—

PREP TIME 2+ HOURS
COOK TIME 5 MINS

I made these a few years back for my family at Christmas time, as the cranberries, nutmeg and spices from the Biscoff biscuits (cookies) are perfect for the festive season. They were such a hit that I was called on to make them again, and now I make them every year and give them as gifts!

150 g (5½ oz) coconut oil or vegan butter, plus extra coconut oil for oiling
300 g (10½ oz) Biscoff biscuits (cookies), or use gluten- or soy-free biscuits
3 tablespoons maple syrup
3 tablespoons brown sugar
3 tablespoons cocoa (unsweetened chocolate) powder
1 teaspoon vanilla extract
100 g (3½ oz/⅔ cup) dried cranberries
1 teaspoon ground cinnamon
pinch of ground nutmeg
grated zest of 1 orange
300 g (10½ oz) vegan dark chocolate with at least 70% cocoa solids, broken into pieces

1. Lightly oil a 20-cm (8-in) square brownie tin (pan) with coconut oil and line with baking parchment.
2. Crush the biscuits into small pieces in a large bowl (I used my hands).
3. Melt the coconut oil or vegan butter with the maple syrup, brown sugar and cocoa powder in a large saucepan over a low heat. Pour the melted mixture into the crushed biscuits along with the vanilla extract, cranberries, cinnamon, nutmeg and orange zest and mix.
4. Spoon the mixture into the prepared brownie tin, pack in and smooth down with the back of a spoon.
5. Melt the vegan chocolate either in the microwave in 20–30-second bursts or in a heatproof bowl set over a saucepan of gently simmering water on the stove, making sure the base of the bowl doesn't touch the water. Pour the melted chocolate over the tiffin mixture in the brownie tin.
6. Leave in the refrigerator for 2 hours, or until set. Once set, dip a knife into boiling hot water and slice the tiffin into bars or squares. Store at room temperature for three to four days, or in the refrigerator for up to a week.

Carrot Cake

One of the tastiest cakes is a carrot cake with the cinnamon, mixed spice, walnuts, incredible icing (frosting) and moist sponge. Traditionally, carrot cake icing has cream cheese, but vegan cream cheese is predominantly made from coconut oil, which behaves differently when whisked as it becomes too runny to work with, so I prefer to use a traditional butter icing for this vegan version as it stays light and fluffy. I've suggested a generous amount but use as much icing as you want on your cake.

SERVES 8-10

—

PREP TIME 20-25 MINS
COOK TIME 35-40 MINS

125 ml (4¼ fl oz/½ cup) vegetable oil
175 g (6 oz/scant 1 cup) light brown sugar
2 teaspoons vanilla extract
300 ml (10 fl oz/1¼ cups) non-dairy milk
375 g (13 oz/3 cups) plain (all-purpose) flour
2 teaspoons baking powder
1½ teaspoons bicarbonate of soda (baking soda)
2 teaspoons ground cinnamon
1 teaspoon mixed spice
½ teaspoon salt
70 g (2½ oz/¾ cup) walnut halves, chopped, plus extra to decorate
4 carrots, about 300 g (10½ oz), grated

FOR THE ICING
250 g (9 oz/2 cups) icing (powdered) sugar
125 g (4½ oz) vegan butter
grated zest and juice of ½ orange
1 tablespoon non-dairy milk

1. Preheat a fan oven to 180°C (400°F). Grease and line a 450 g (1 lb) loaf tin (pan) with baking parchment.
2. Whisk the oil, sugar and vanilla extract together in a large bowl for a few minutes until the sugar starts to dissolve, then stir in the milk.
3. Sift in the flour, baking powder, bicarbonate of soda, cinnamon, mixed spice and salt, and gently combine. Stir in the walnuts and grated carrot.
4. Spoon the batter into the greased and lined loaf tin and bake in the oven for 35–40 minutes until a skewer inserted into the centre of the cake comes out clean.
5. Leave the cake to cool in the tin for 5–10 minutes, then turn out onto a wire rack to cool completely.
6. Meanwhile, for the icing (frosting), sift half the icing sugar into a large bowl, add the butter and beat with a whisk until light and fluffy. Whisk in the remaining icing sugar, half the orange zest and all of the orange juice and milk by hand or with an electric whisk until light and smooth.
7. Spread the icing over the top of the cake (it's fine if a little runs down the sides). Sprinkle the top with the remaining grated orange zest and chopped walnuts. Store for three to four days at room temperature, or in the refrigerator for up to a week.

SWEETS & BAKING

MAKE IT VEGAN

Caramel Truffles

MAKES 12–15
—
PREP TIME 1½–2 HOURS
COOK TIME 1–2 MINS

Chocolatey, caramelly and creamy, this recipe only requires a few simple ingredients. The Medjool dates create a delicious caramel sweet centre, the almond butter brings a buttery texture, and the dark chocolate coating mixed with the sea salt brings all the flavours together in a dreamy truffle.

200 g (7 oz) Medjool
  dates, stoned
2 tablespoons almond butter
  or peanut butter
2 good pinches of sea salt

FOR THE COATING
100 g (3½ oz) vegan dark
  chocolate with at least
  70% cocoa solids, broken
  into pieces
pinch of sea salt
2 teaspoons coconut oil

1. Blitz the dates, almond or peanut butter and sea salt in a food processor until smooth. Scrape out into a medium bowl and freeze for about 30 minutes to harden.
2. Line a large baking sheet with baking parchment or a silicone sheet.
3. When the date mixture is cooled, remove from the freezer. Pinch out a small amount of the mixture and roll between your hands to make truffle balls about 2 cm (¾ in) in diameter. Arrange on the lined baking sheet and freeze again for 30 minutes to harden.
4. Add the chocolate to a heatproof bowl and microwave in 30-second bursts until melting. Make sure you keep checking and stirring the chocolate after 30 seconds, so it doesn't overheat. Alternatively, melt on the stove in a heatproof bowl set over a saucepan of simmering water, making sure the bottom of the bowl doesn't touch the water. Add the coconut oil and stir through.
5. Remove the balls from the freezer and, using a fork, dip them into the melted chocolate, then place back on the lined baking sheet. Leave to set for 5–10 minutes (until they're very nearly set), then sprinkle the top with a few grains of sea salt. Leave to set completely for a further 10–15 minutes, and enjoy. Store in an airtight container for three to four days, or in the refrigerator for up to a week.

Choc a Choc Chocolate Cake

This cake is filled with chocolate! The more chocolate the better when it comes to dessert for me, and chocolate cake has always been my favourite since childhood.

SERVES 12

—

PREP TIME 20 MINS
COOK TIME 35 MINS

150 g (5½ oz) vegan butter, plus extra for greasing
300 ml (10 fl oz/1¼ cups) non-dairy milk
2 tablespoons apple cider vinegar
3 tablespoons apple sauce (shop-bought is fine)
300 g (10½ oz/scant 2½ cups) self-raising (self-rising) flour
200 g (7 oz/generous ¾ cup) golden caster (superfine) sugar
100 g (3½ oz/generous ¾ cup) cocoa (unsweetened chocolate) powder
1 teaspoon instant coffee powder (optional)
1 teaspoon baking powder
1 teaspoon bicarbonate of soda (baking soda)
1 teaspoon vanilla extract
pinch of table salt

FOR THE CHOCOLATE BUTTERCREAM
100 g (3½ oz) vegan dark chocolate with at least 70% cocoa solids, chopped into pieces
200 g (7 oz) vegan butter
400 g (14 oz/3¼ cups) icing (powdered) sugar
100 g (3½ oz/generous ¾ cup) cocoa (unsweetened chocolate) powder
pinch of salt
1 tablespoon non-dairy milk

TO DECORATE
grated vegan dark chocolate with at least 70% cocoa solids or vegan chocolate sprinkles
fresh raspberries or slices of strawberries

1. Preheat a fan oven to 170°C (375°F). Grease two 20 cm (8 in) sandwich tins (pans) all over with vegan butter, then line the bases with baking parchment.
2. Pour the milk into a medium bowl and add the vinegar. Wait five minutes for the mixture to begin turning lumpy and split.
3. Add all the remaining cake ingredients to a large bowl, pour over the milk and vinegar mixture, and whisk until smooth. Divide the batter evenly between the prepared tins and bake in the oven for 25–30 minutes until a skewer inserted into the centre of the cakes comes out clean. Leave to cool in the tins for 5–10 minutes, then turn onto wire racks to cool completely.
4. To make the buttercream, add the chocolate to a heatproof bowl and microwave in 30-second bursts until melting. Alternatively, melt on the stove in a heatproof bowl set over a saucepan of simmering water, making sure the bottom of the bowl doesn't touch the water. Make sure you keep checking and stirring the chocolate after 30 seconds, so it doesn't overheat. Leave to cool for a few minutes.
5. Beat the vegan butter and icing sugar together in a large bowl with a wooden spoon until light and fluffy. Sift in the cocoa powder and salt, then pour in the melted chocolate and milk and mix until smooth.
6. Spread half the buttercream on top of one of the cooled sponges and sandwich the cakes together. Spread the remaining buttercream over the top and down the sides of the cake. Decorate with some grated chocolate and fresh berries. The cake will store in an airtight container for three to four days.

Alex's Bread

At the start of lockdown Alex got into bread making. It became his new obsession (and I reaped the benefits). I've shared it on my YouTube channel many, many times, so I couldn't leave it out of my first cookbook. Not only is it simple, but it is also so much better than any bread you can buy in the supermarket. Plus, after much experimentation Alex has found an easy way to make it work every time.

MAKES 1 LOAF

—

PREP TIME 2½–3 HOURS
COOK TIME 30-35 MINS

250 g (9 oz/2 cups) strong white bread flour, plus extra for dusting
250 g (9 oz/2 cups) plain (all-purpose) flour
7 g (¼ oz) packet of fast-action dried yeast
7 g (¼ oz) salt
325 ml (11 fl oz/1⅓ cups) water
50 g (1¾ oz/scant ½ cup) mixed seeds, plus 20 g (¾ oz/2½ tablespoons) seeds for sprinkling

1. Add the flours, yeast and salt to a stand mixer fitted with a dough hook attachment, making sure that the yeast and salt don't touch by adding to opposite sides of the bowl.

2. Add the measured water and mix on a medium speed for 5 minutes, or until you have a smooth dough. While the mixer is still running, add the seeds. Peel the dough off the hook and leave in the bowl.

3. If you're not using a mixer, add the flours, yeast and salt to a large bowl and mix together with your hands. Turn the dough out onto a lightly floured work surface and knead well for 5 minutes. Using the palm of your hands, make an indent in the middle of the dough, then lift the dough up at the top and press back down into the indent. Rotate and repeat for 5 minutes until a smooth dough is formed. Sprinkle over the mixed seeds and knead a little more until the seeds are evenly incorporated. Return the dough to the bowl.

4. Cover the dough with a dish towel and leave to rise in a warm spot for 1–1½ hours until doubled in size.

5. Turn the dough out onto a lightly floured work surface and gently flatten ready to fold. To create a ball, pinch the edge furthest away from you and fold over, almost to the other side (about three-quarters of the way). Rotate and repeat, continuing to turn and fold the dough all the way around until you have a ball of dough that's bouncy. Flip the dough so the seams are on the bottom, cover with a dish towel and leave to rest for 30 minutes.

6. Turn the ball of dough back over so the seams are on the top again and flatten. Pinch at ten and two o'clock and fold each of these points over into the middle (one on top of the other) to form a triangle shape. Starting at the pointy top, roll the dough down into a tight sausage shape, then sprinkle over the remaining seeds.

7. Line a large baking tray (pan) with baking parchment or a silicone sheet. Transfer the dough to the lined baking tray, cover with a dish towel and leave to rest for another 30 minutes.

8. Meanwhile, preheat a fan oven to 200°C (425°F). Add 100 ml
   (3½ fl oz/scant ½ cup) of boiling water to a roasting tin or baking
   tray and place in the base of the oven.
9. Once risen, score the bread with a sharp knife diagonally and evenly
   three times across the top, then bake in the oven for 30 minutes until
   golden brown.
10. Remove from the oven, transfer to a wire rack and leave to cool for
    20–30 minutes. The bread is best eaten the same day but can be
    stored for up to three to four days.

About
the Author

Madeleine Olivia is a full-time content creator whose aim is to make it easy and attainable for anyone looking to live a more plant-based lifestyle. She provides her 550,000 YouTube subscribers with delicious, simple and affordable vegan recipes and is the author of Minimal, and ebooks Versatile Vegan and Plant Kitchen Comforts.

Acknowledgements

This book wouldn't have been made without my incredible publishers, Hardie Grant, and my Editor Kate Burkett. They came to me and asked to publish a vegan cookbook with enthusiasm and passion for this project. It has been my ultimate career dream and they have enabled me to make this dream into a reality. The support I have received throughout the creation of this book from Kate has been incredible, and I couldn't have done it without her.

This book wouldn't have been the same without working on it with my biggest food inspiration, my mum Debbie. We planned this project together, combing through her massive cookbook collection for inspiration, writing long lists of ideas, creating different recipes together and testing them endlessly. She taught me how to cook growing up, and as someone who isn't vegan, she gave me a new perspective and input into what readers would need from this book. *Make It Vegan* was a collaboration between us and I am endlessly grateful for her input.

Thank you to Clare Winfield, my inspiring photographer who captured all of my recipes beautifully throughout the book, and Ali at Alexandra House Studios, my best friend and an incredibly talented photographer, for the fantastic cover image.

Thank you to Libby Silbermann for styling the recipes to make them look seriously delicious and Florence, Caitlin and Olivia for their support and work on the shoot for this cookbook.

Thank you to my designer Lucy Sykes-Thompson at Studio Polka for making this book as stunning as it is. And thank you to Laura Eldridge and Ruth Tewskbury for putting this book out to the world.

A huge thank you to my team and family at home; Charlie and Tom, the best sister and brother-in-law I could ask for, for managing, supporting and helping me from the very start of this project. Thank you to my husband Alex, and father, Mick for always being there for me.

And a final and huge thank you to my audience, for watching my videos, subscribing and following, for making my recipes and for buying this book. You made this cookbook a reality, and I hope you have loved it as much as I have loved creating it for you.

Index

Published in 2023 by Hardie Grant Books,
an imprint of Hardie Grant Publishing

Hardie Grant Books (London)
5th & 6th Floors
52–54 Southwark Street
London SE1 1UN

Hardie Grant Books (Melbourne)
Building 1, 658 Church Street
Richmond, Victoria 3121

hardiegrantbooks.com

British Library Cataloguing-in-Publication
Data. A catalogue record for this book
is available from the British Library.

Make it Vegan
ISBN: 9781784886448

10 9 8 7 6 5 4 3 2 1

Publishing Director: Kajal Mistry
Senior Commissioning Editor: Kate Burkett
Design: Studio Polka
Photography: Clare Winfield (internals) and Ali Green (cover)
Photographer's assistant: Caitlin Dalgetty
Food and prop stylist: Libby Silbermann
Food stylist's assistants: Florence Blair and Olivia Abdoo
Copy Editor: Kathy Steer
Proofreader: Caroline West
Indexer: Cathy Heath
Production Controller: Katie Jarvis

Colour Reproduction by p2d
Printed and bound in China
by Leo Paper Products Ltd